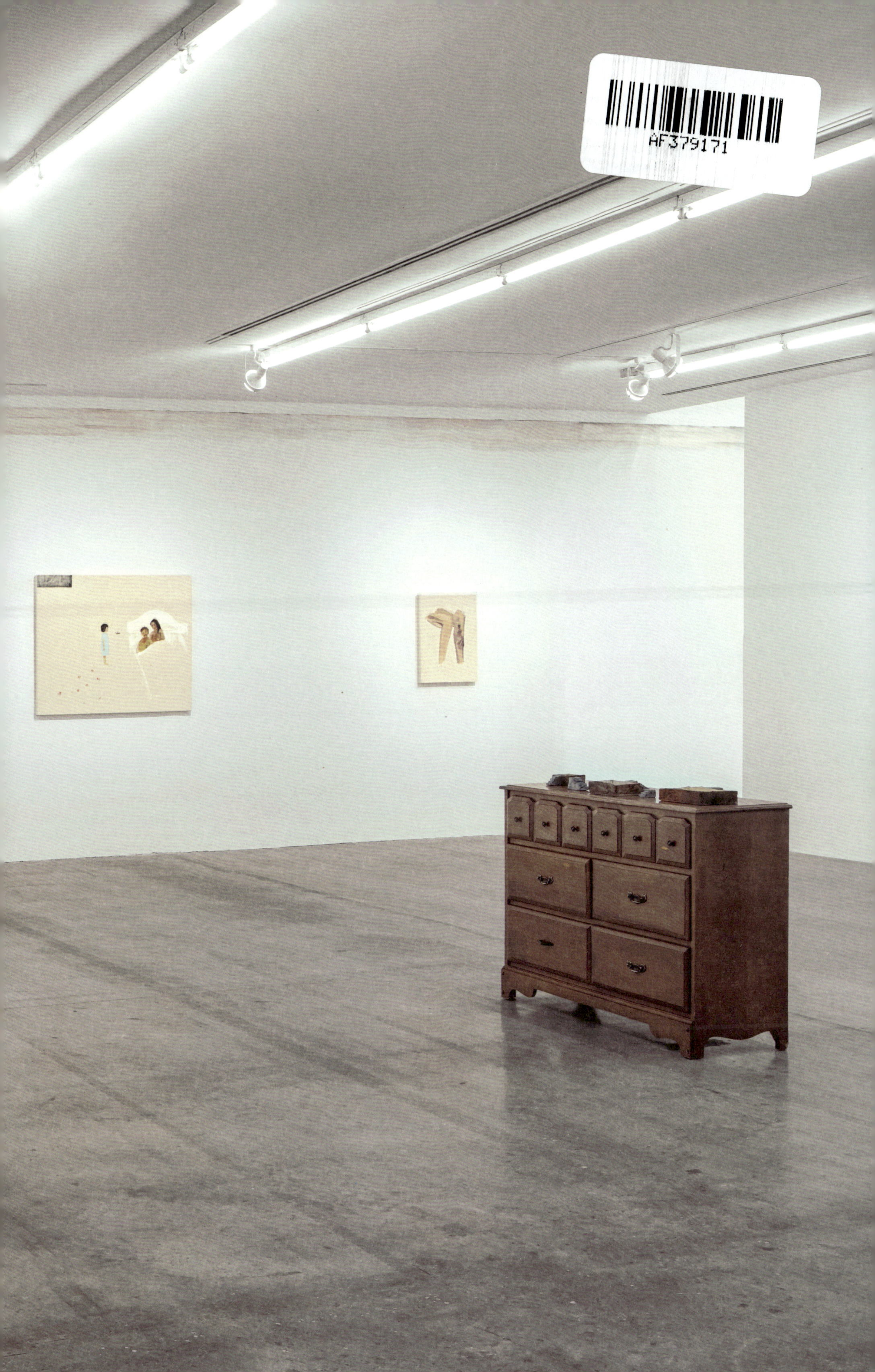

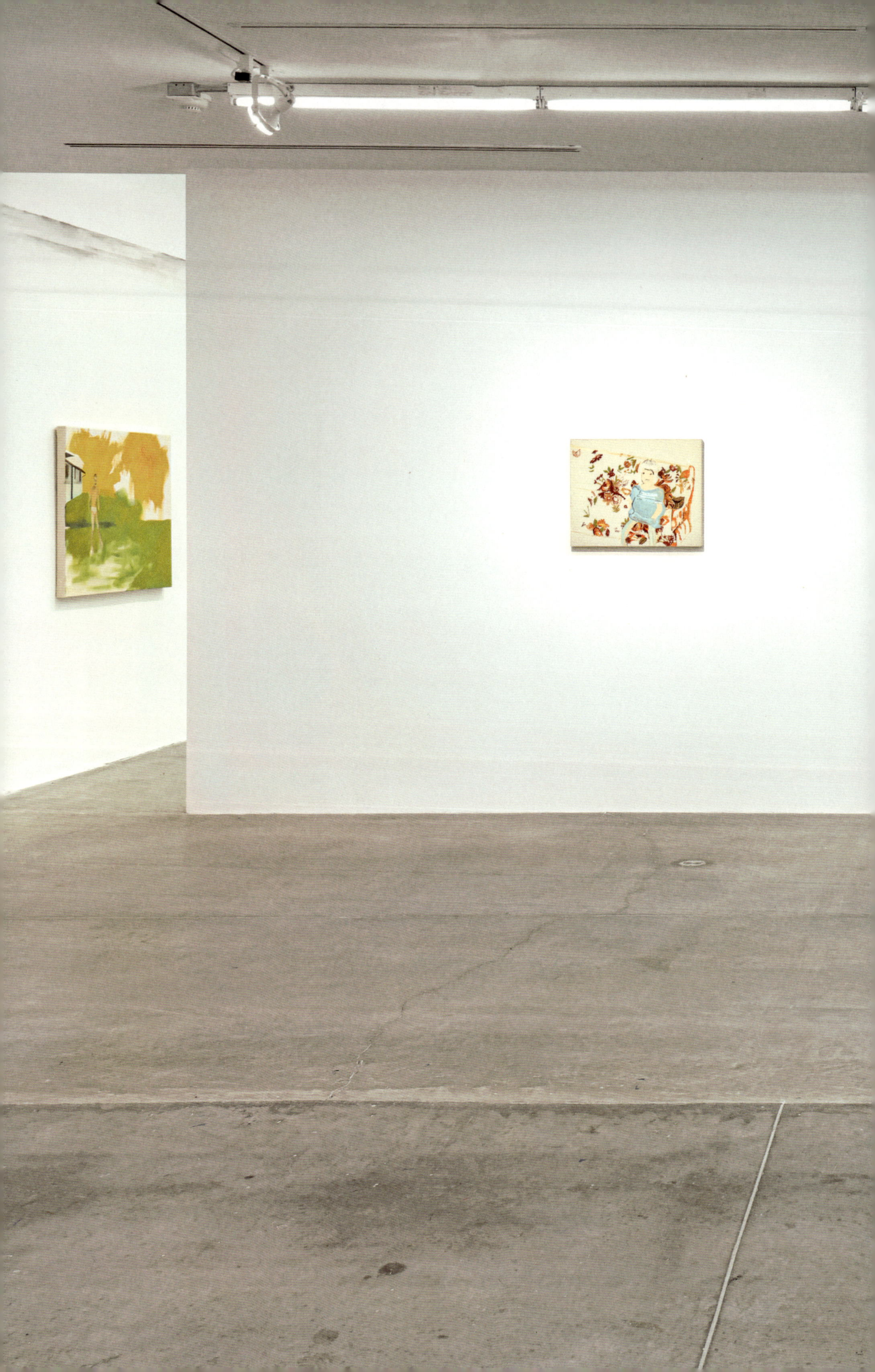

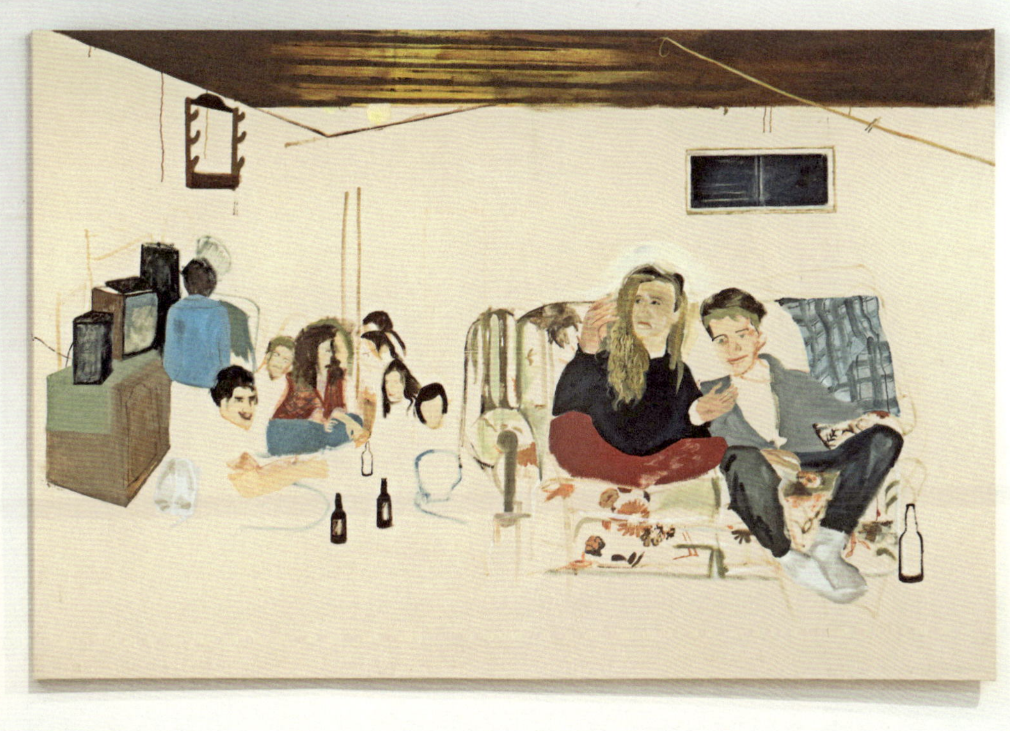
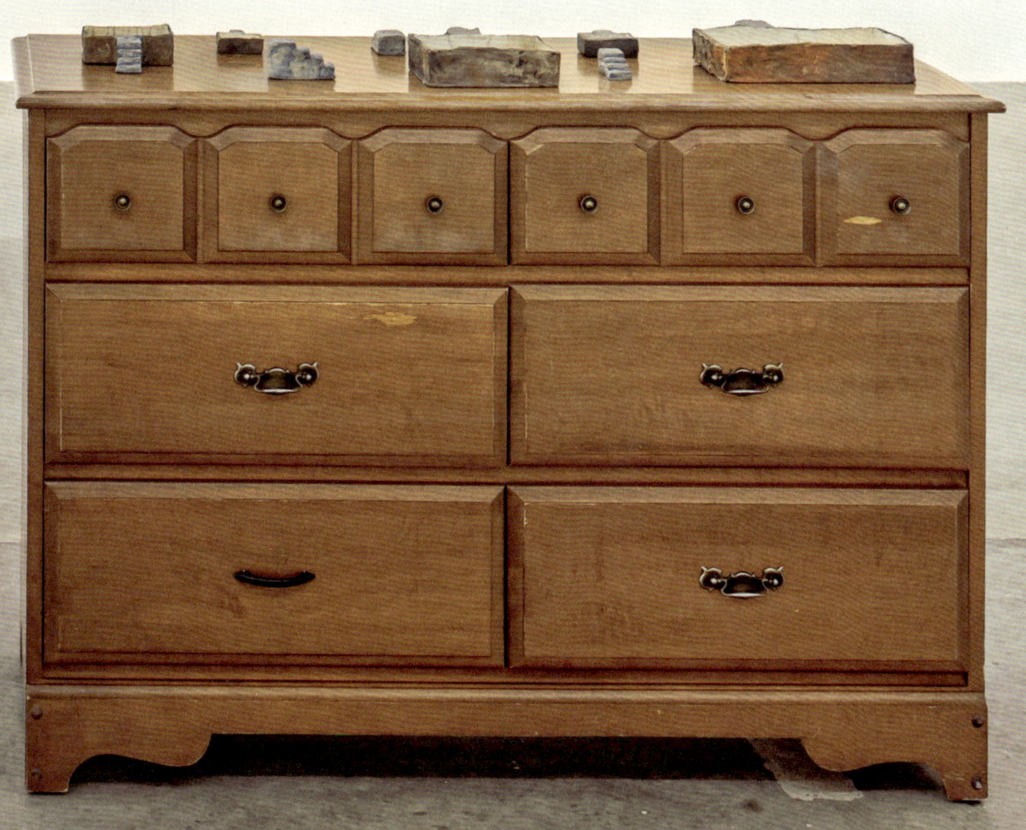

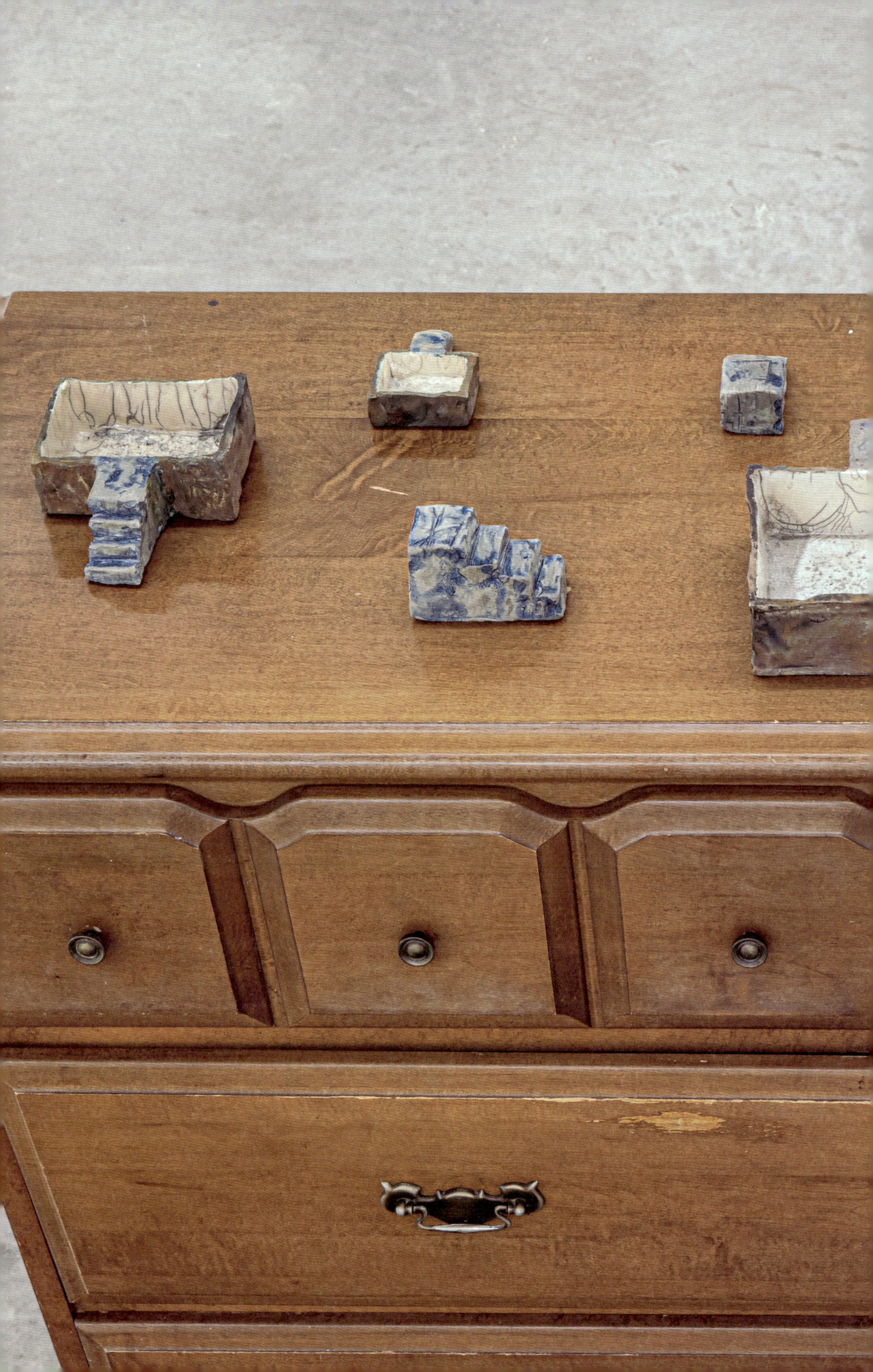

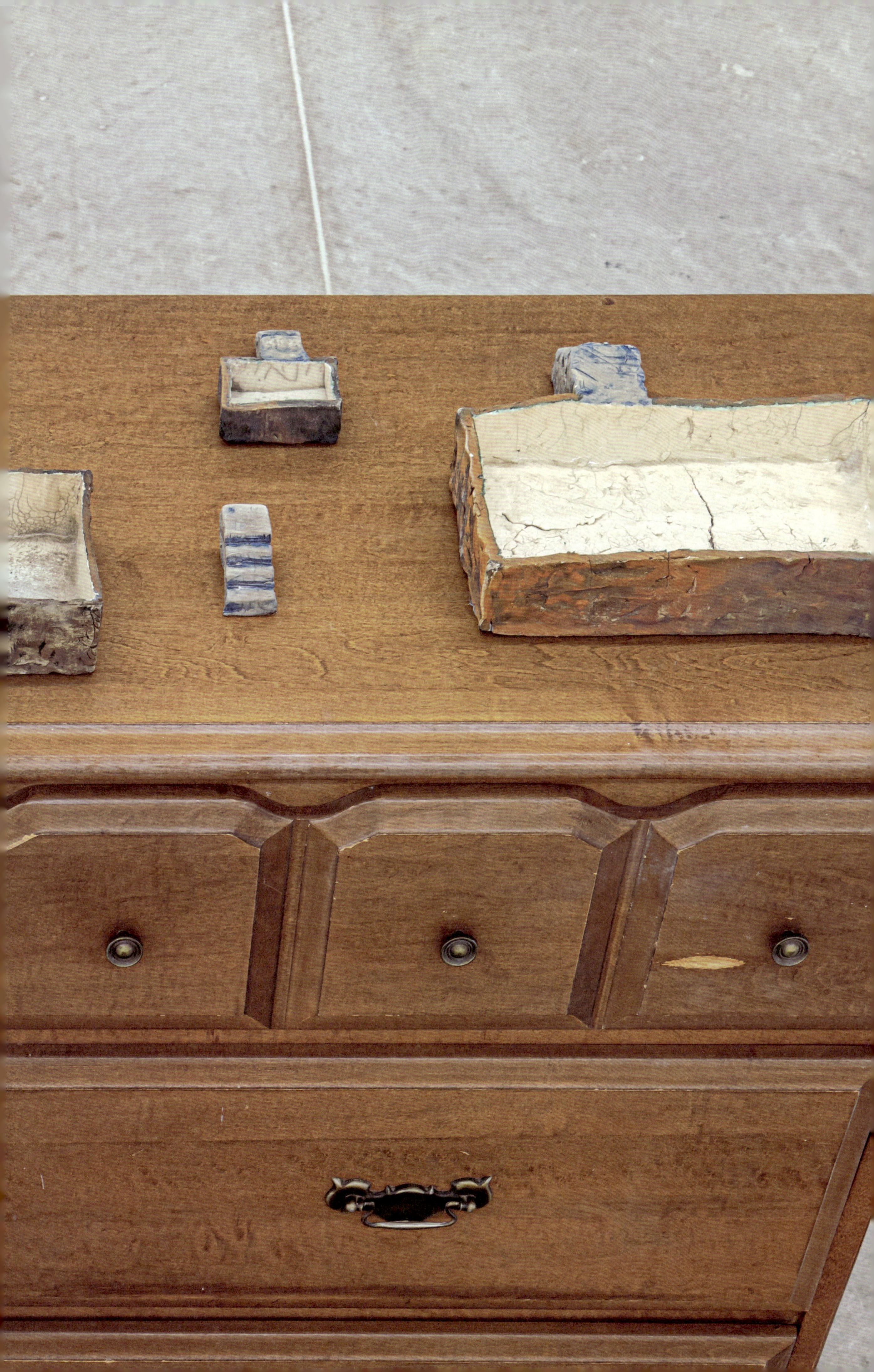

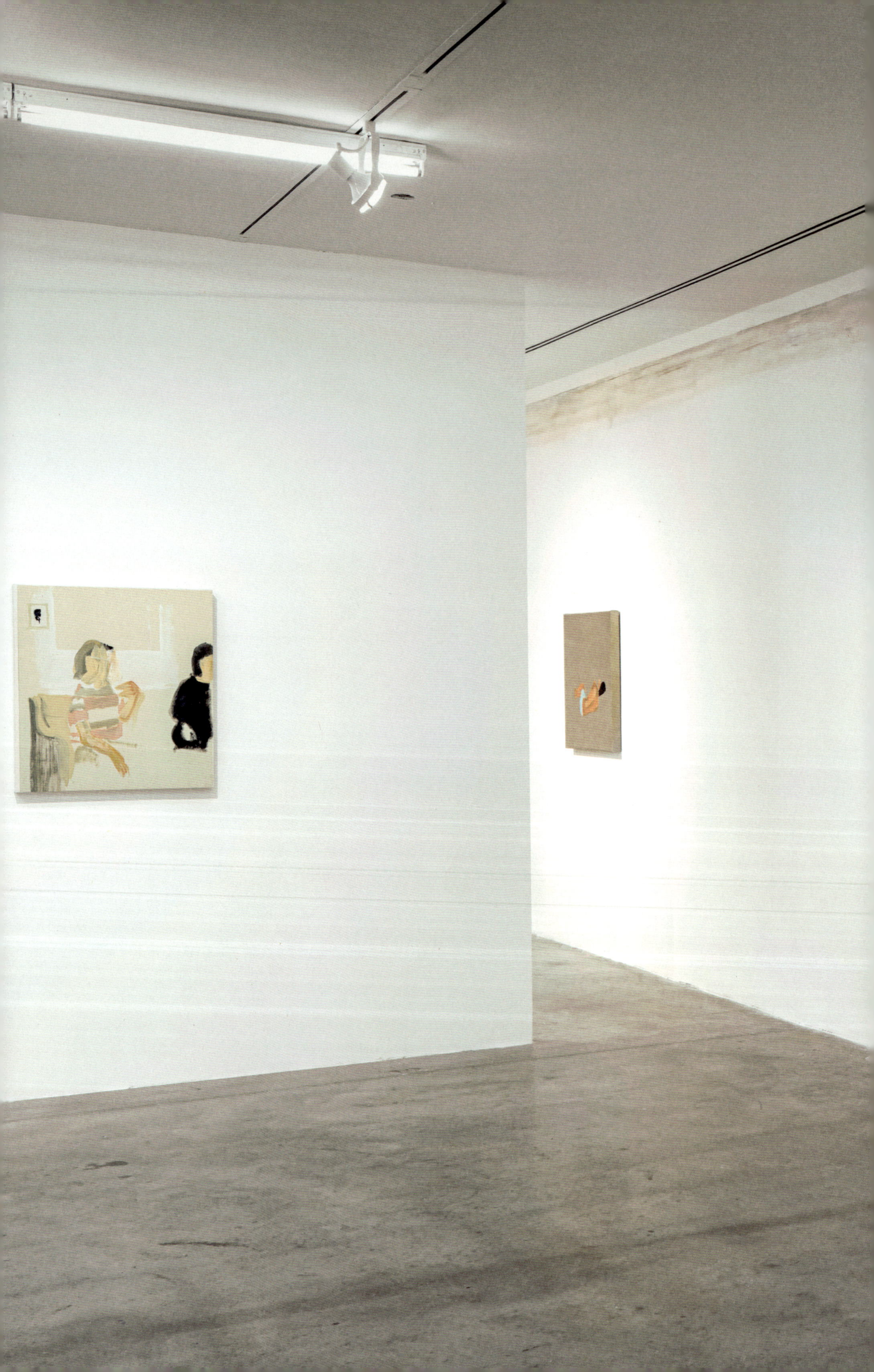

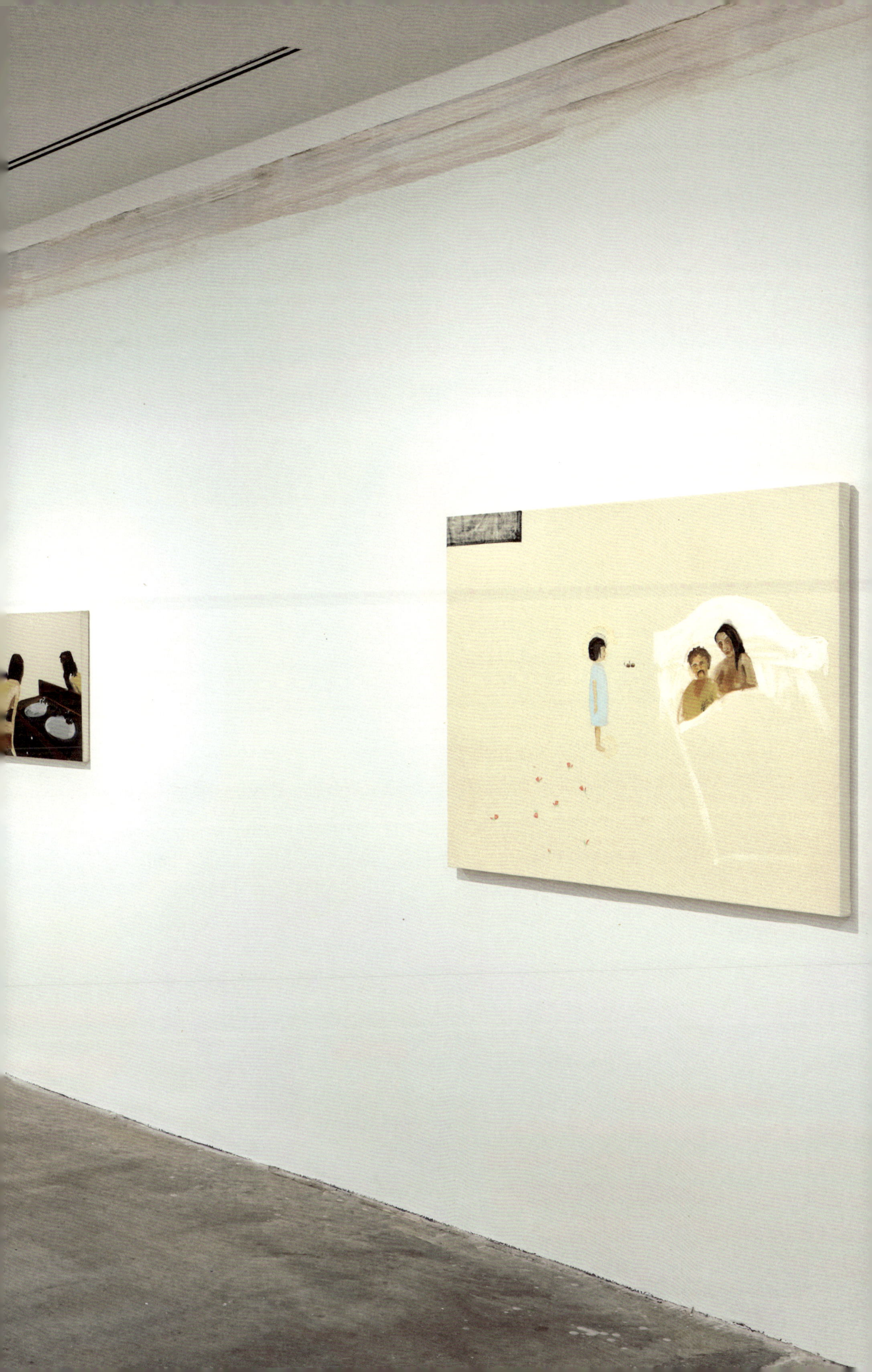

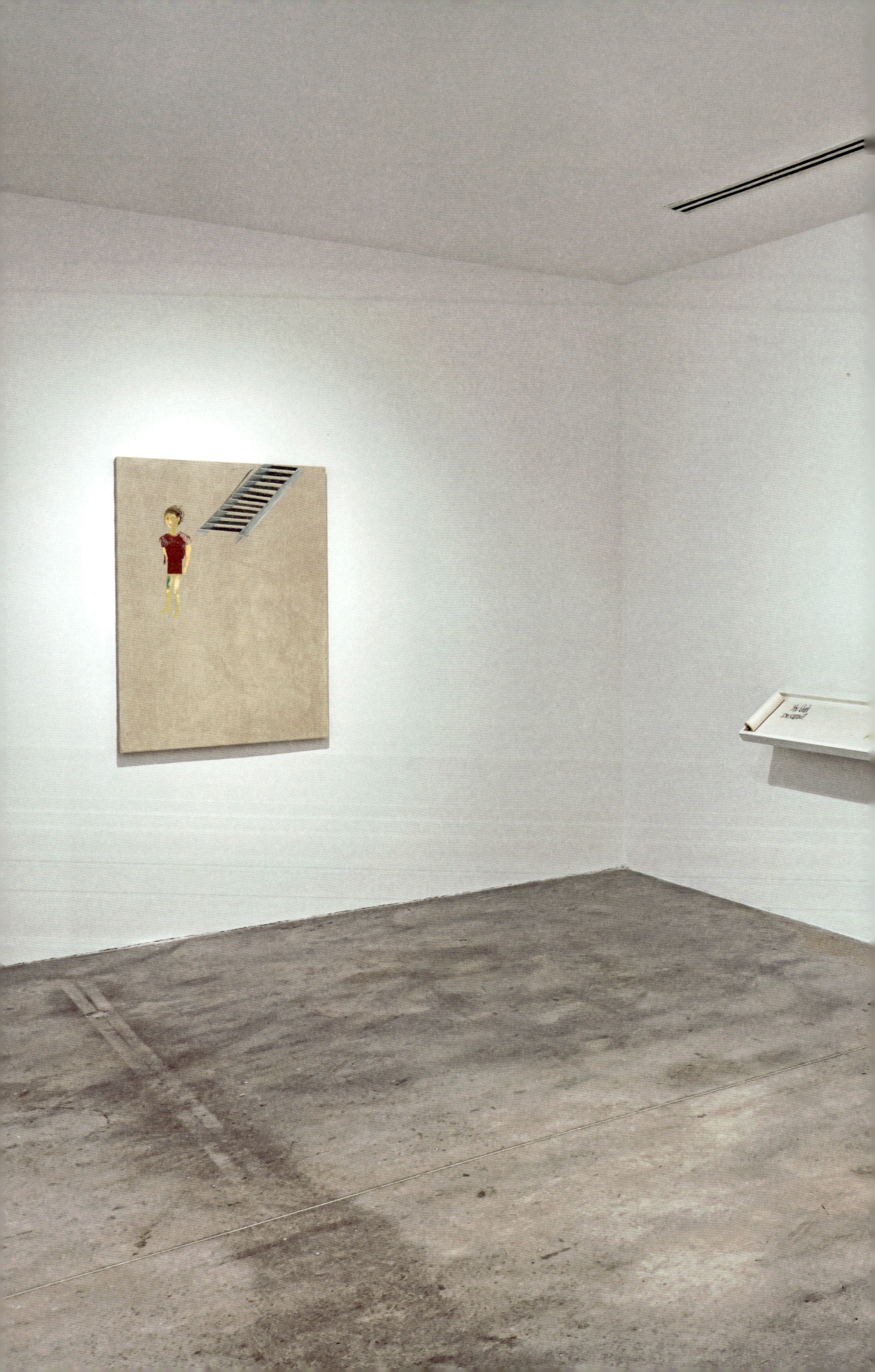

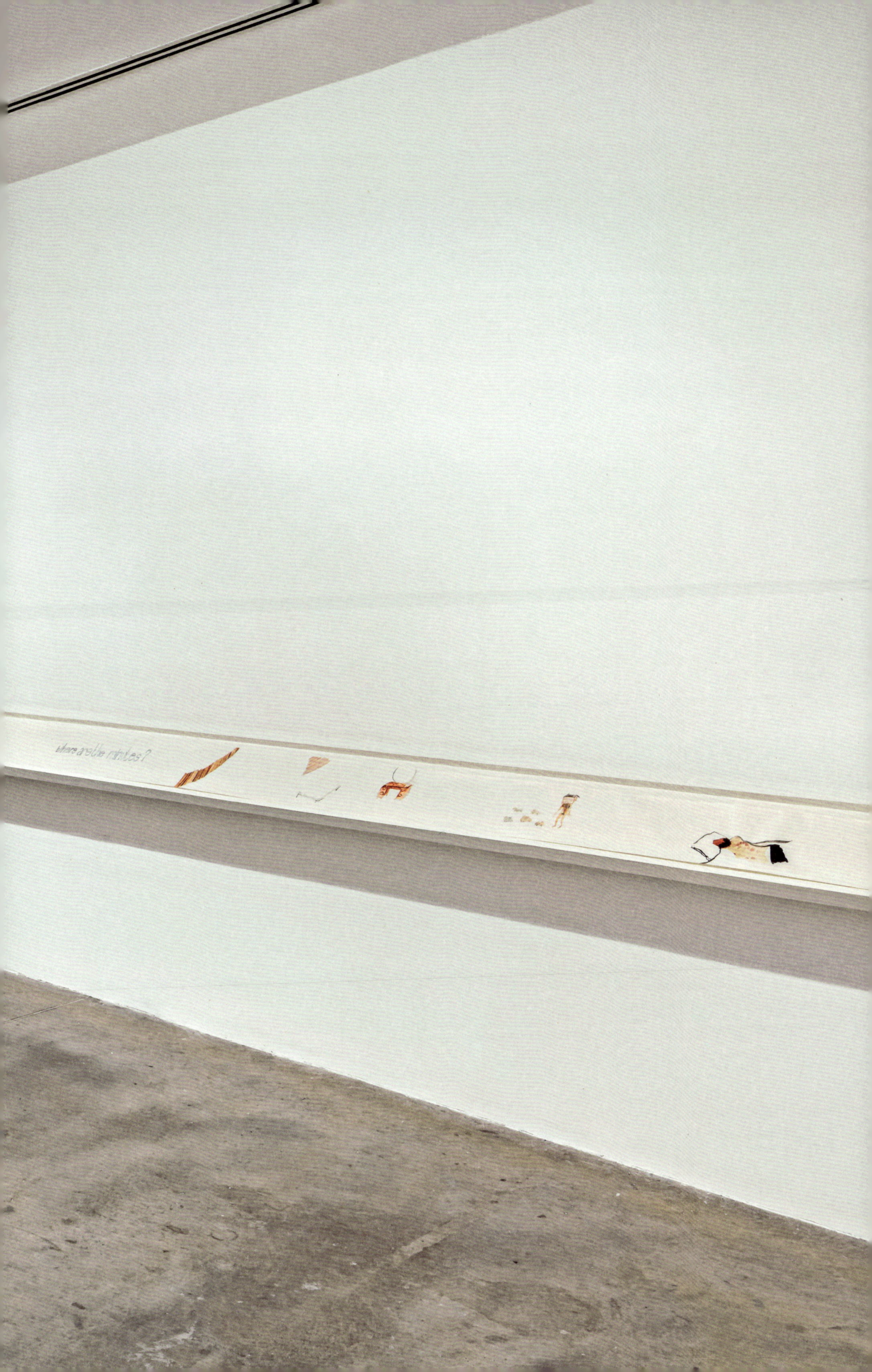
where are the rules?

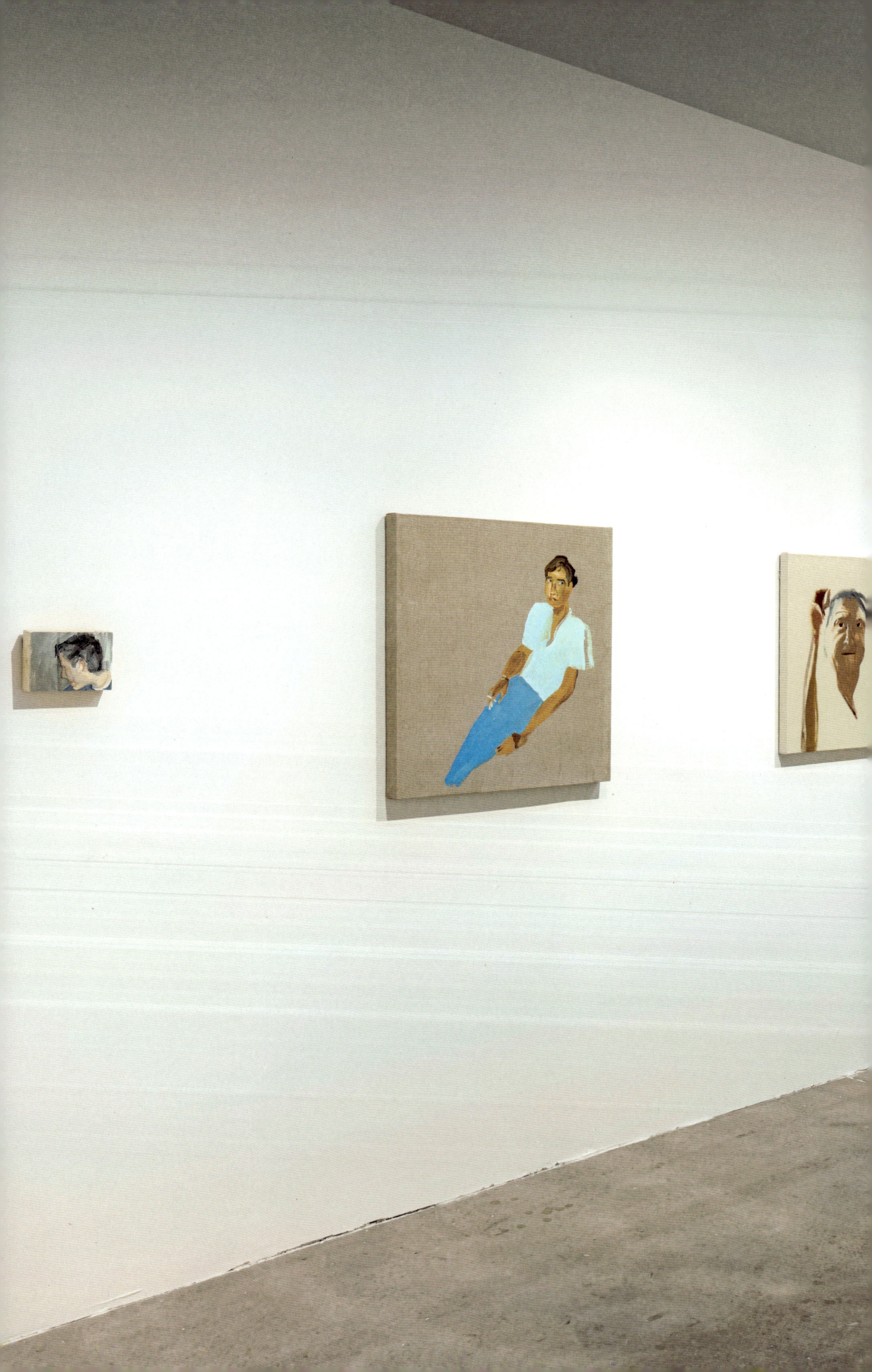

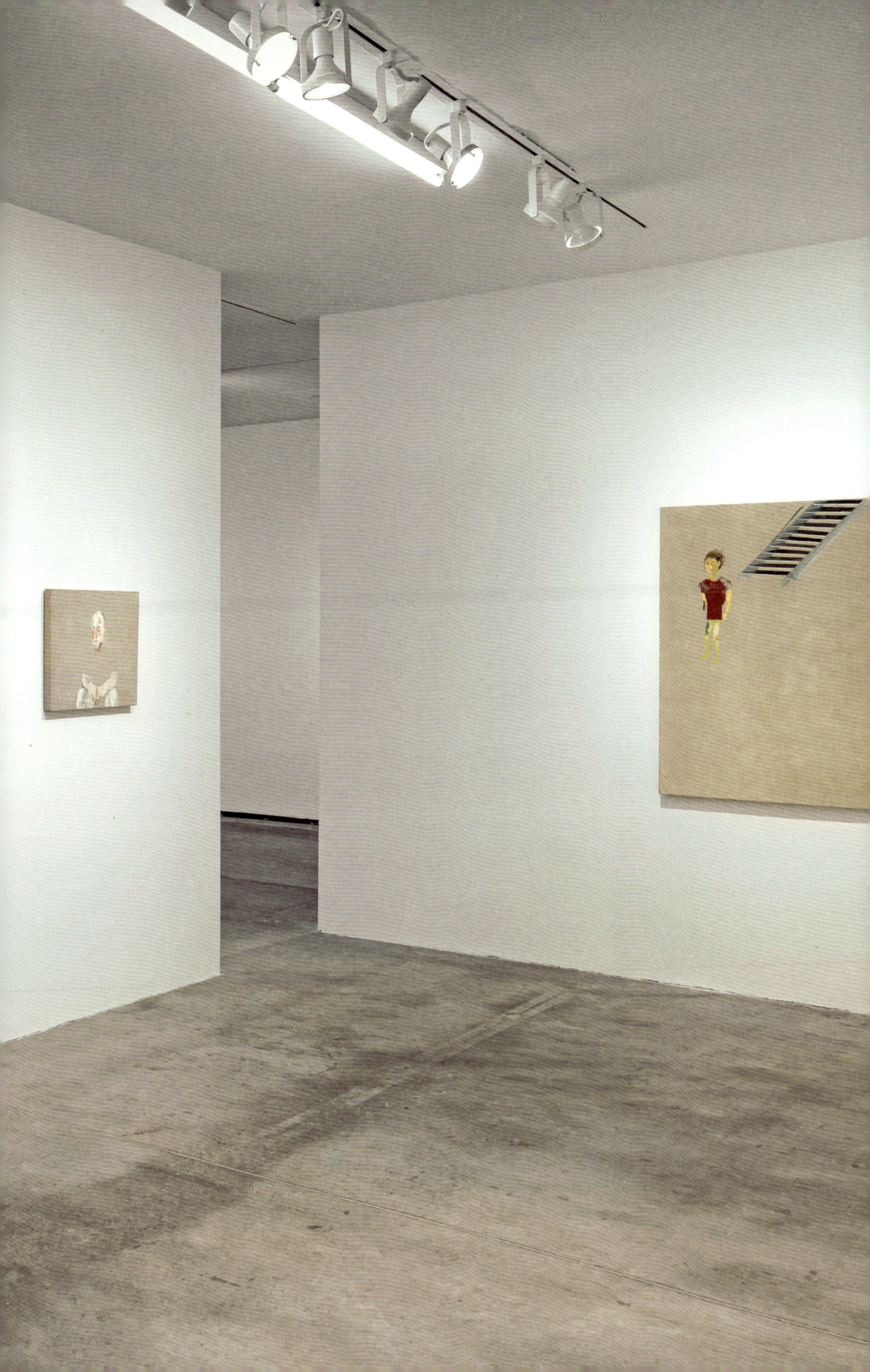

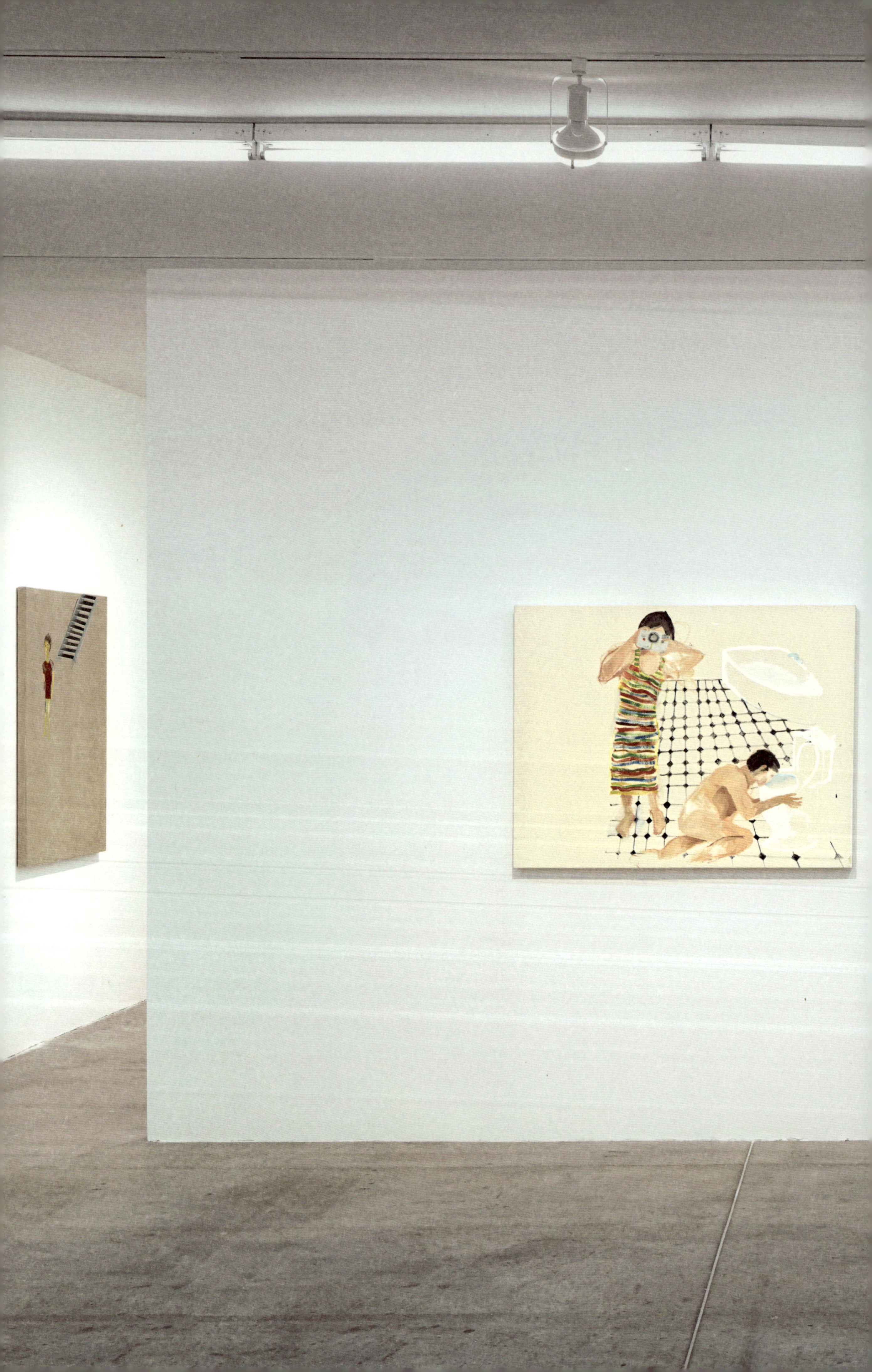

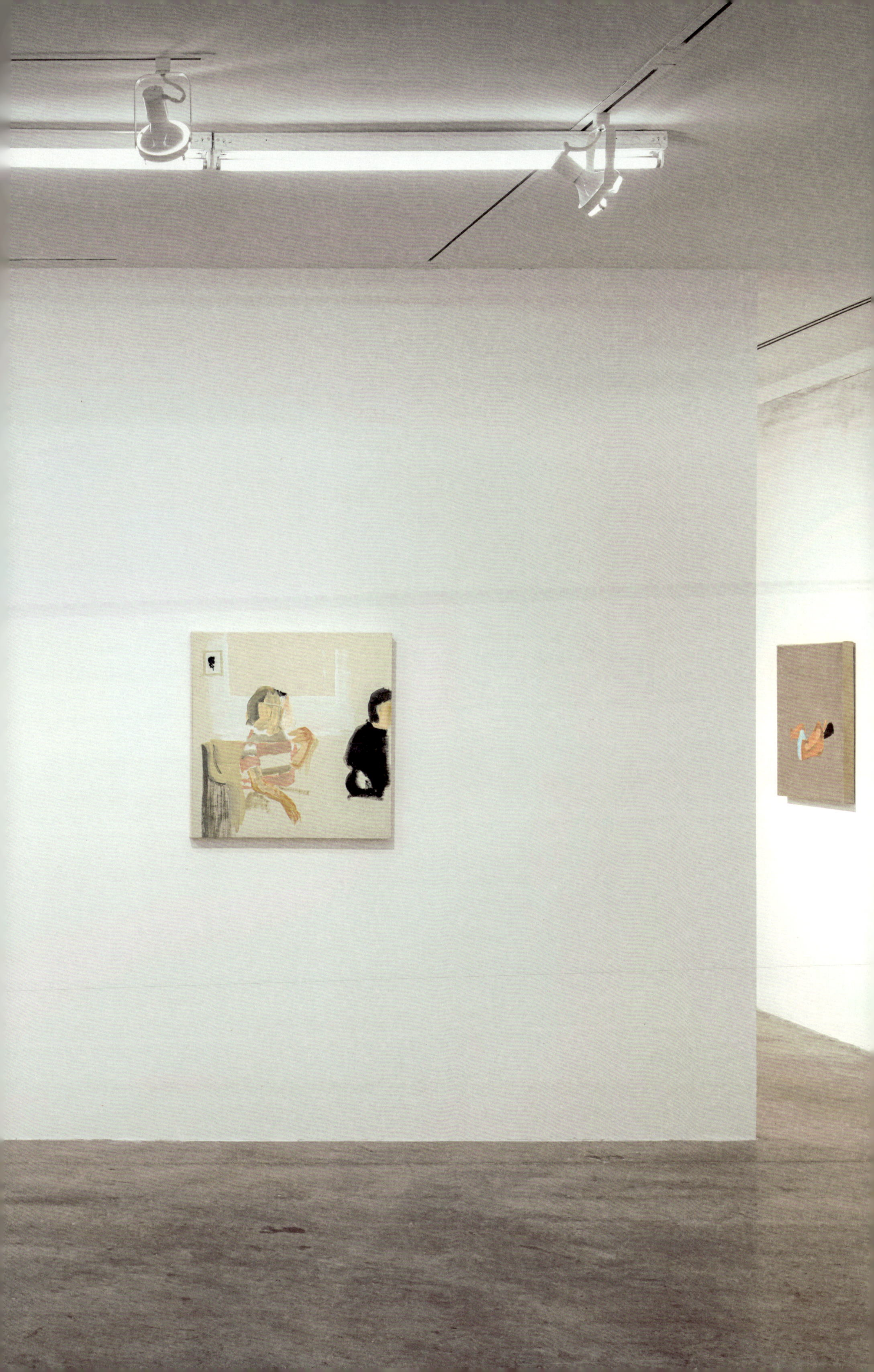

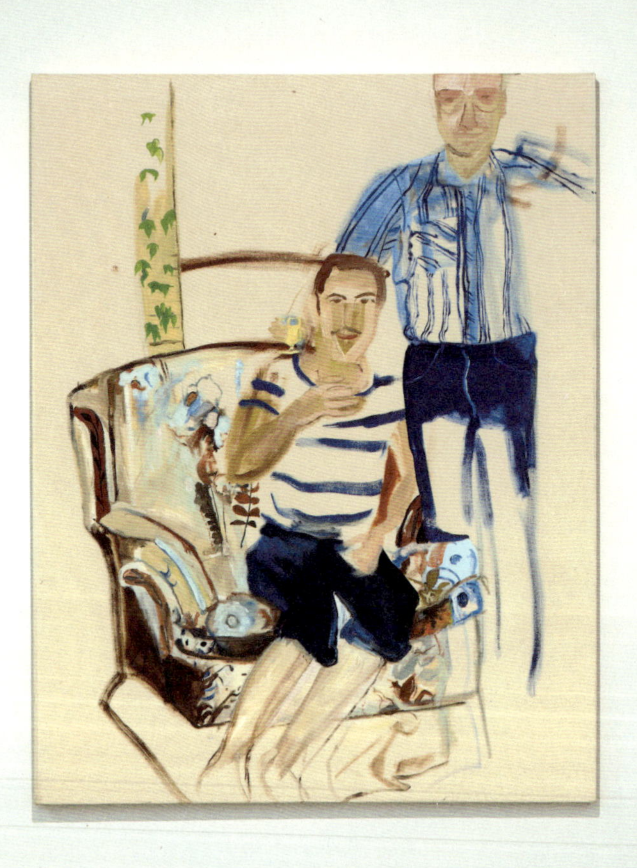

BRENDA DRANEY

DRINK FROM THE RIVER

TABLE OF CONTENTS

ACKNOWLEDGEMENTS

This publication documents the exhibition *Drink from the river* by
Brenda Draney, which was organized and circulated by The Power
Plant Contemporary Art Gallery, Toronto, curated by Jacqueline Kok,
and presented February 3–May 14, 2023. *Drink from the river* then
travelled to The Arts Club of Chicago, June 14–August 15, 2023; and
the Art Gallery of Alberta (AGA), Edmonton, January 22–May 8, 2024.

The Power Plant, The Arts Club of Chicago, and the Art Gallery
of Alberta offer our heartfelt thanks to Brenda Draney for accepting
our invitation to host *Drink from the river* across our many institutions. We are also grateful to the publication's contributors—Graham
Foy, David Garneau, Jacqueline Kok, Ken Lum, and Souvankham
Thammavongsa—for their thought-provoking texts. We would like
to extend our deep appreciation to Markus Weisbeck and his team
at Studio Markus Weisbeck for their thoughtful publication design,
and to our co-publishers at Hatje Cantz for their interest in distrib-
uting this book. Thank you also goes to The Power Plant's long-time
copy editor, Jack Stanley, for his consistent attention to detail, and
to The Power Plant's Publications Officer, Claudia Tavernese, for
her unwavering dedication to this project.

The Arts Club of Chicago acknowledges the Smart Family
Foundation for its core support of the Ambition Fund, which makes
possible significant international engagements such as this. We are
grateful to our colleagues at The Power Plant for their collegiality
and collaboration. At The Arts Club, we thank Administrative Assis-
tant Mia Morettini, Communications Manager David Merz, Programs
Director Jenna Lyle, Finance Manager James Lucchesi, and especially Gallery Director Adam Mikos for stewarding all aspects of this
project with keen attention and care.

The Art Gallery of Alberta would like to acknowledge the
dedicated efforts of our staff, with special thanks for the realiza-
tion of the exhibition in Edmonton to: Exhibitions Manager Sara
McKarney, Creative Director Charles Cousins, Lead Preparator
Jesse Dutton-Kenny, Senior Preparator Clint Wilson, and Preparator
Kevin Sehn. We are also grateful to all members of the AGA team
for their contributions. In addition, the Art Gallery of Alberta is grateful for the support of its public funders: the Edmonton Arts Council
and the City of Edmonton, the Alberta Foundation for the Arts, and
the Canada Council for the Arts, whose contributions make our
exhibitions, publications, and programs possible. It is a great plea-
sure for the AGA to host this exhibition in amiskwacîwâskahikan,
Brenda Draney's hometown, in Treaty 6 territory.

The Power Plant is deeply grateful to its team: Head of Curatorial Affairs Adelina Vlas, Registrar Julie Anne, Head of Installation
and Facilities Paul Zingrone, Head of Public Programs and Outreach
Muna Cann, Head of Communications and Marketing Beverly Cheng,
Head of Development William Craddock, and Finance Manager
Celia Salas, among many other colleagues. A special thank you
to *Drink from the river* curator and former Bill Morneau and Nancy
McCain Curatorial Fellow, 2021–23, Jacqueline Kok, for her curatorial vision.

We express our heartfelt thanks to the touring venues who committed funds to the production of this catalogue, The Arts Club of Chicago and the Art Gallery of Alberta. The Power Plant also extends its gratitude to publication supporters Rob and Monique Sobey and the Müller family, and to touring partner the Canada Council for the Arts. Special thanks to Catriona Jeffries for her constant support throughout the exhibition and publication process.

Thank you to those who graciously lent their works to the exhibition, including Gage and Luke Allard, John Cook, Michelle Koerner and Kevin Doyle, Zita Cobb, the Art Gallery of Alberta Collection, the Indigenous Art Collection, Crown-Indigenous Relations and Northern Affairs Canada, the Payne-Moran Collection, Alex Hass, Joe Friday and Grant Jameson, Vicki and Bruce Heyman, and lenders who wish to remain anonymous. The Power Plant also receives significant, sustained support from the Canada Council for the Arts, the Ontario Arts Council, the Toronto Arts Council, the Ontario Trillium Foundation, the Ontario Cultural Attractions Fund, and Harbourfront Centre. Additionally, BMO Financial Group supports our *ALL YEAR, ALL FREE* initiative, which ensures the gallery remains accessible to the public, free of charge.

Catherine Crowston
Executive Director and Chief Curator, Art Gallery of Alberta

Janine Mileaf
Executive Director and Chief Curator, The Arts Club of Chicago

Carolyn Vesely
Interim Director, The Power Plant Contemporary Art Gallery

When encountering Brenda Draney's paintings for the first time, one may be struck by their affective solitude. In Draney's exhibition *Drink from the river*, the artist engages with this quietness in sincere and evocative ways. By placing ordinary moments at the forefront of her paintings, she draws attention to the politics of intimacy as shaped by memory, community, trauma, and healing.

Draney's largest institutional exhibition to date, *Drink from the river* features both newly commissioned and recent paintings, as well as several small-scale sculptures. Inside the gallery space, memories of specific moments are presented alongside one another, inviting viewers into a charged yet private setting. These moments, while particular to the artist, also carry universal visual cues and codes, which connect them to shared human experience. Draney's works thus encourage audiences to actively exercise empathy as a muscle; by bridging the private with the public, *Drink from the river* makes room for viewers to consider the nuances of intimacy as an emotional anchor around which a sense of self and community is built.

Drink from the river gathers paintings that convey a sense of experience specific to Draney's First Nations community, both past and present. The exhibition's title points toward the irony of an expression that indicates spiritual plenitude and connection to greater forces, even as it references instances of inundation. Paintings like *Flood*, 2009, and *Evacuation*, 2013, make explicit reference to catastrophic events, while others such as *Toast*, 2022, capture an instance of casual camaraderie. The metaphorical reference to powerful waters that are at once sustaining and destructive is carried into the works that depict intimacy and joy, as well as those that mark social class or hardship. Throughout the exhibition, there are signs of Draney's wit and sophisticated take on the entirety of her experience. The sofa with a floral motif that recurs in a number of works, for example, is made in the Colonial Revival style, a name which unwittingly references the oppression of those who settle into its lumps and curves.

Using words to introduce an oeuvre marked by silence necessarily involves a compromise. The poignancy of Draney's paintings lies in their evocative capacity rather than in explanation, and yet some attempt to specify is warranted. Expanses of white space in these works suggest not incompletion but an invitation to connect. At the same time, those unspoken elements relate to the functions of memory in which certain vignettes contain detail and clarity, while others fade. Here, silence is not only inherent to the medium of painting, but it is operative in Draney's imaginary. Narratives of gathering, relationship, trauma, history, family, Indigeneity, and confrontation suggest themselves in Draney's deft strokes, but the details of character, event, and location remain open and available to the viewer. Draney's paintings remind us that visual art offers an alternative to language, even if the imagery points toward a story.

Drink from the river includes six new paintings commissioned by The Power Plant that expand on Draney's research concerning the intersection of horror and intimacy. Taking on this motif allowed the artist to continue exploring her stylistic approach of leaving substantial blank spaces on her canvases, a gesture that is not only part of an art-historical legacy with regard to what a painting means or looks like but also invites the audience to develop a reciprocal relationship with the conveyed images. In Draney's canon, blank spaces are opportunities—chances to give voice to unspoken moments and untranslatable memories. In these new works from 2022, Draney looks at how traces of traumatic events can be found in a bruise, a couch, a ceiling fan. Her stark and direct denotation of these seemingly mundane things parallels a socio-political system that privileges some individuals over others. Who is implicated in events? When does a memory become traumatic? And how does it continue to influence our everyday lives?

We would like to thank all who accepted our invitation to take part in this publication, especially the contributing authors: filmmaker Graham Foy, artist and academic David Garneau, *Drink from the river* curator Jacqueline Kok, artist and academic Ken Lum, and poet and author Souvankham Thammavongsa. Their texts dive into the intersection of the artist's experience growing up as a contemporary Indigenous person and the human experience of unpacking and confronting trauma. Lum and Kok offer formal readings of the artist's works that analyze the ways in which Draney appropriates the art historical canon in order to disrupt it and reference various theorists and philosophers to suggest the impetus behind such decisions. Thammavongsa's and Foy's essays, which are more personal responses to Draney's works, demonstrate the generative powers that lie in quotidian moments and their related memories. Lastly, Garneau's text explores how Draney's oeuvre resonates with those who share a common place of origin and, particularly, how the legacy of colonialism affects both Indigenous and settler subjects. In bringing these seemingly disparate voices together, this publication demonstrates the cohesive power of Draney's practice: by leaning into our own uncomfortable memories, we are able to see how they can be unifying in myriad ways—in public and private spaces, and across cultures and generations.

Our heartfelt thanks go to Brenda Draney for her trust in our institutions. This exhibition and publication would not have been possible without her perseverance and dedication. By exploring everyday spaces and emotions, Draney invokes a quiet contemplation and renders visible those tentative moments that mark us in resounding ways as we navigate socio-economic realities. She creates space for a kind of vulnerability whose complexities are given the poetic justice they deserve. Draney's works are captivating, as if prompting viewers to dive into deep retrospection. In doing so, they mirror the values of The Power Plant and The Arts Club of Chicago—the desire to start conversations that will generate a more holistic sense of kinship and community building. We hope this exhibition and publication will inspire audiences to empathize with those whose worlds might differ from their own, even if ever so slightly.

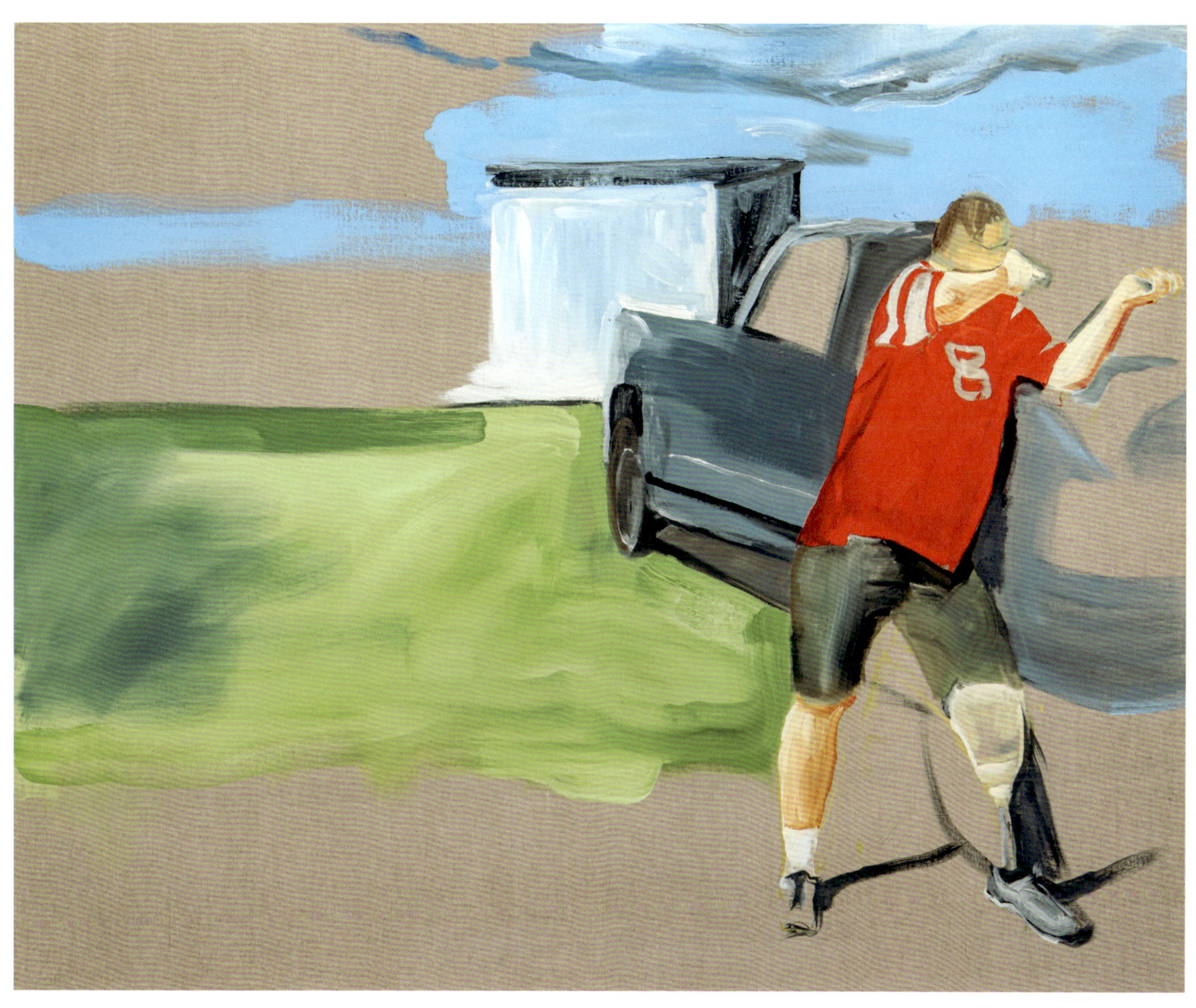

.30-.30
2013

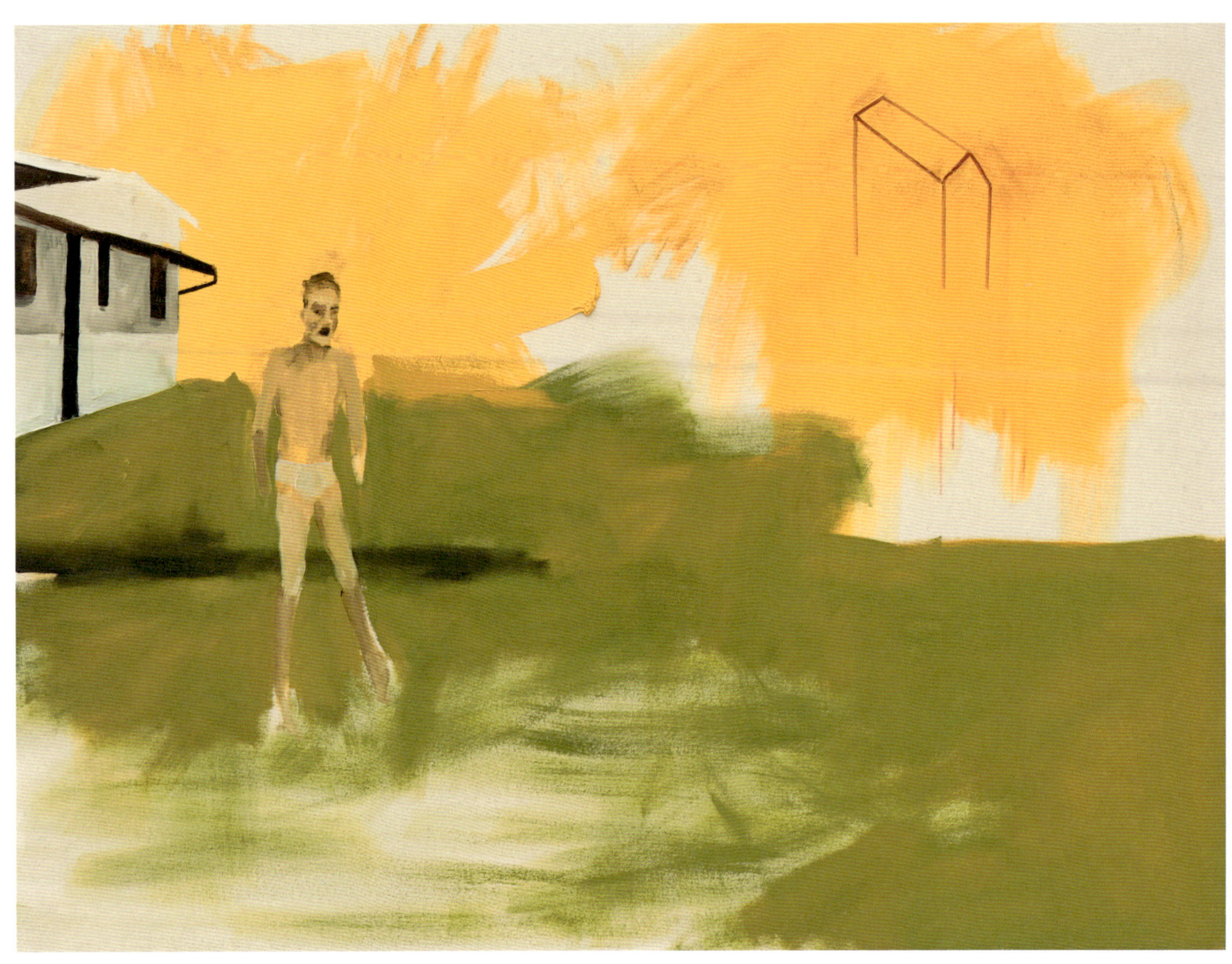

Evacuation
2013

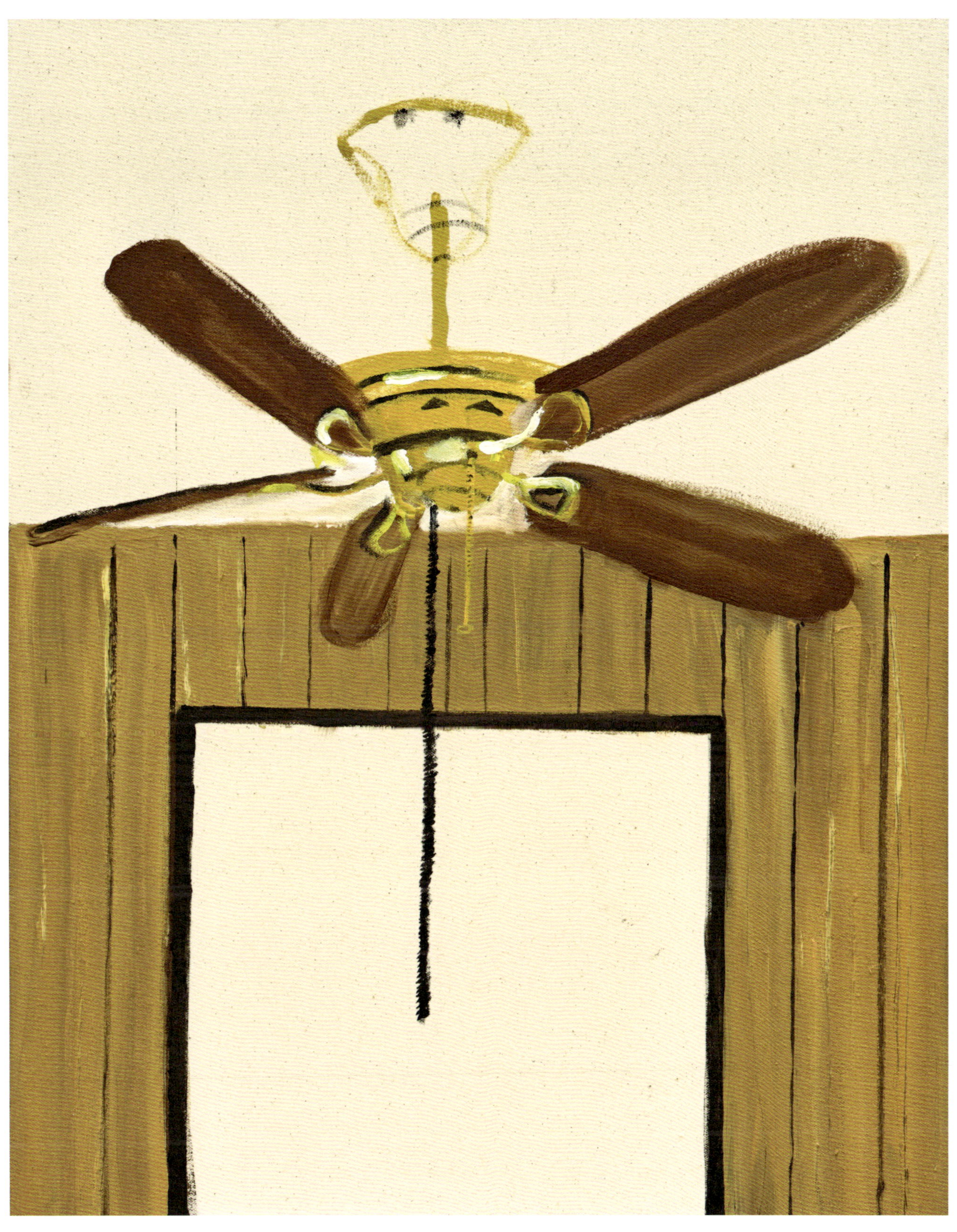

Cut
2022

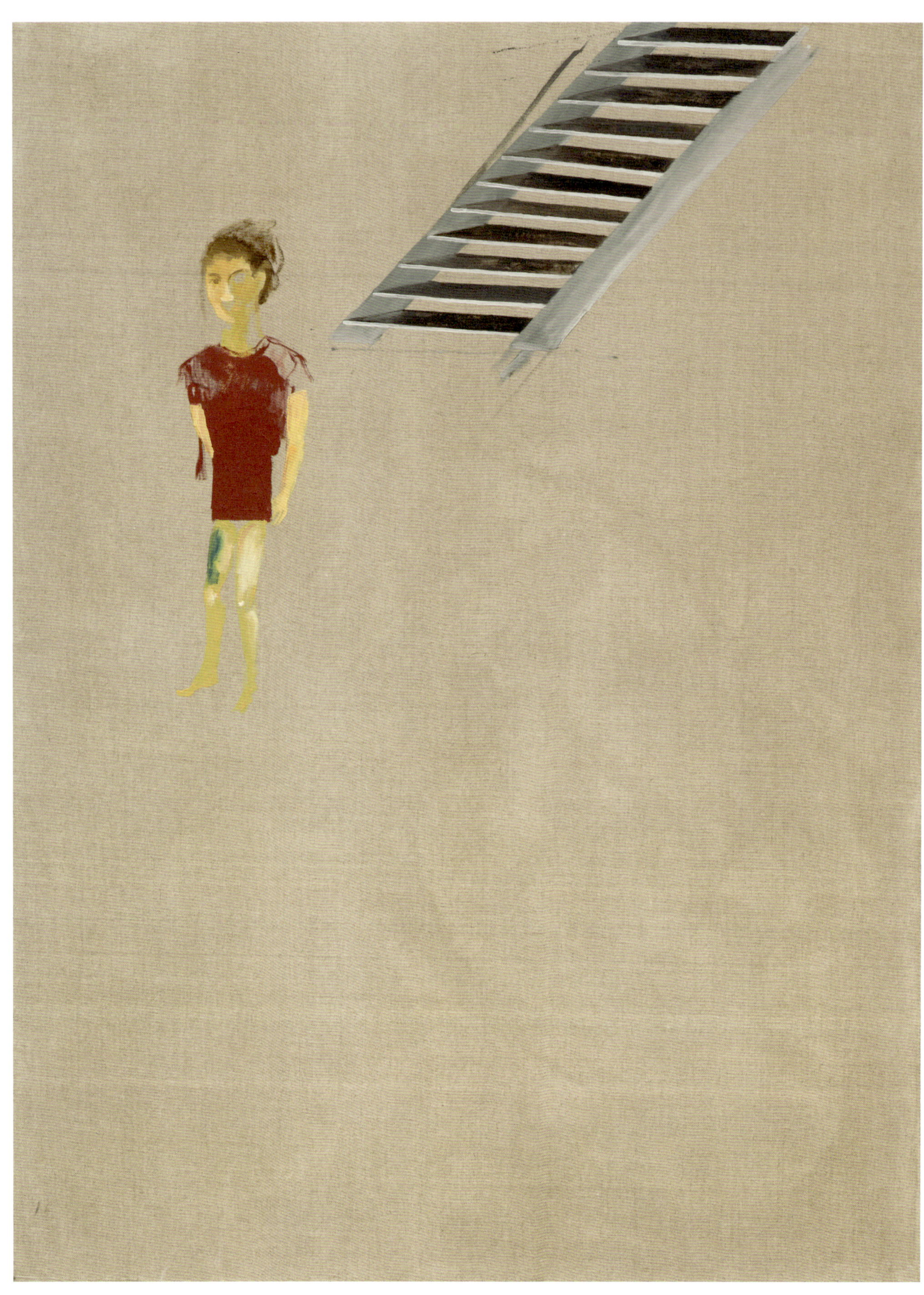

Descendant
2013

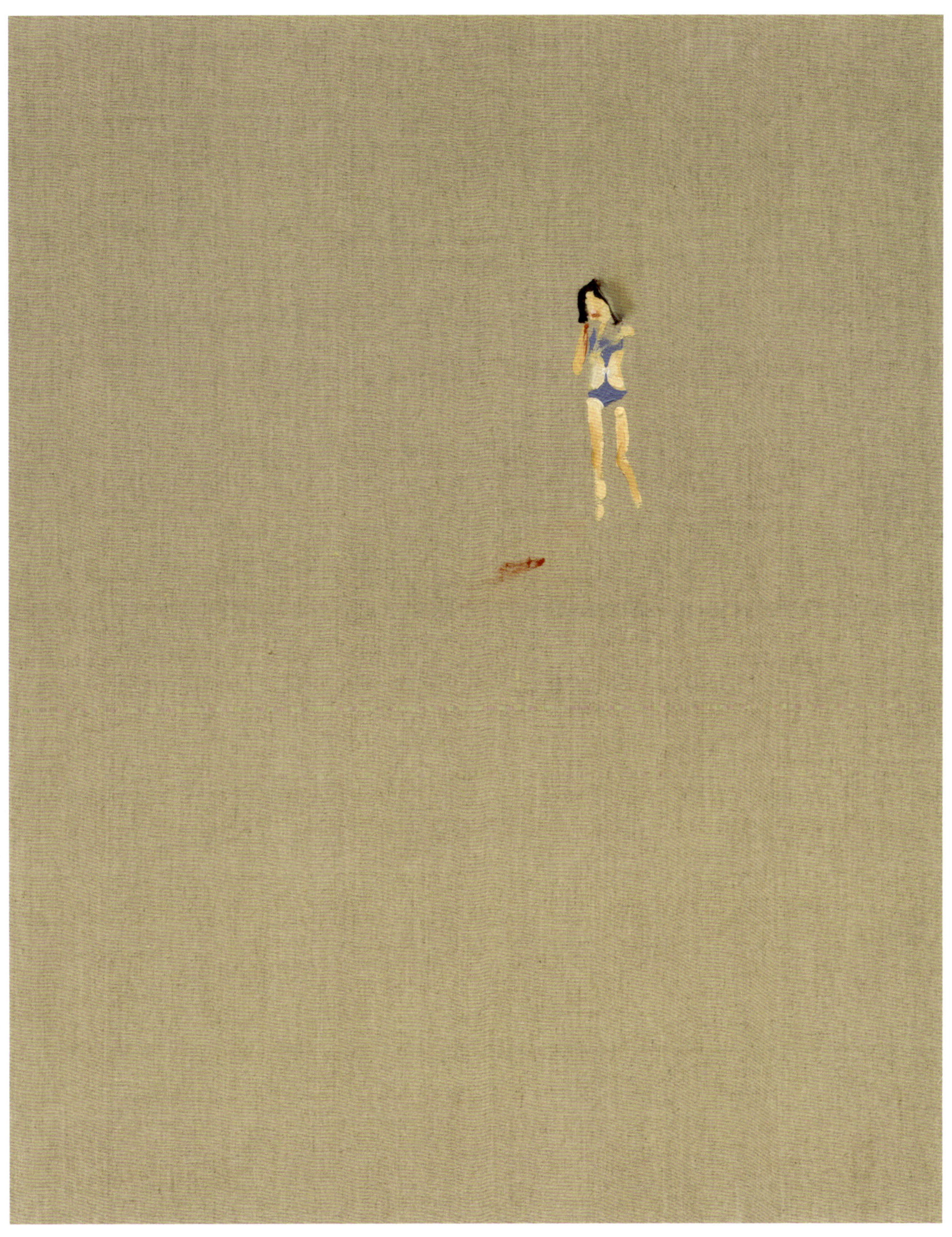

Julie
2010

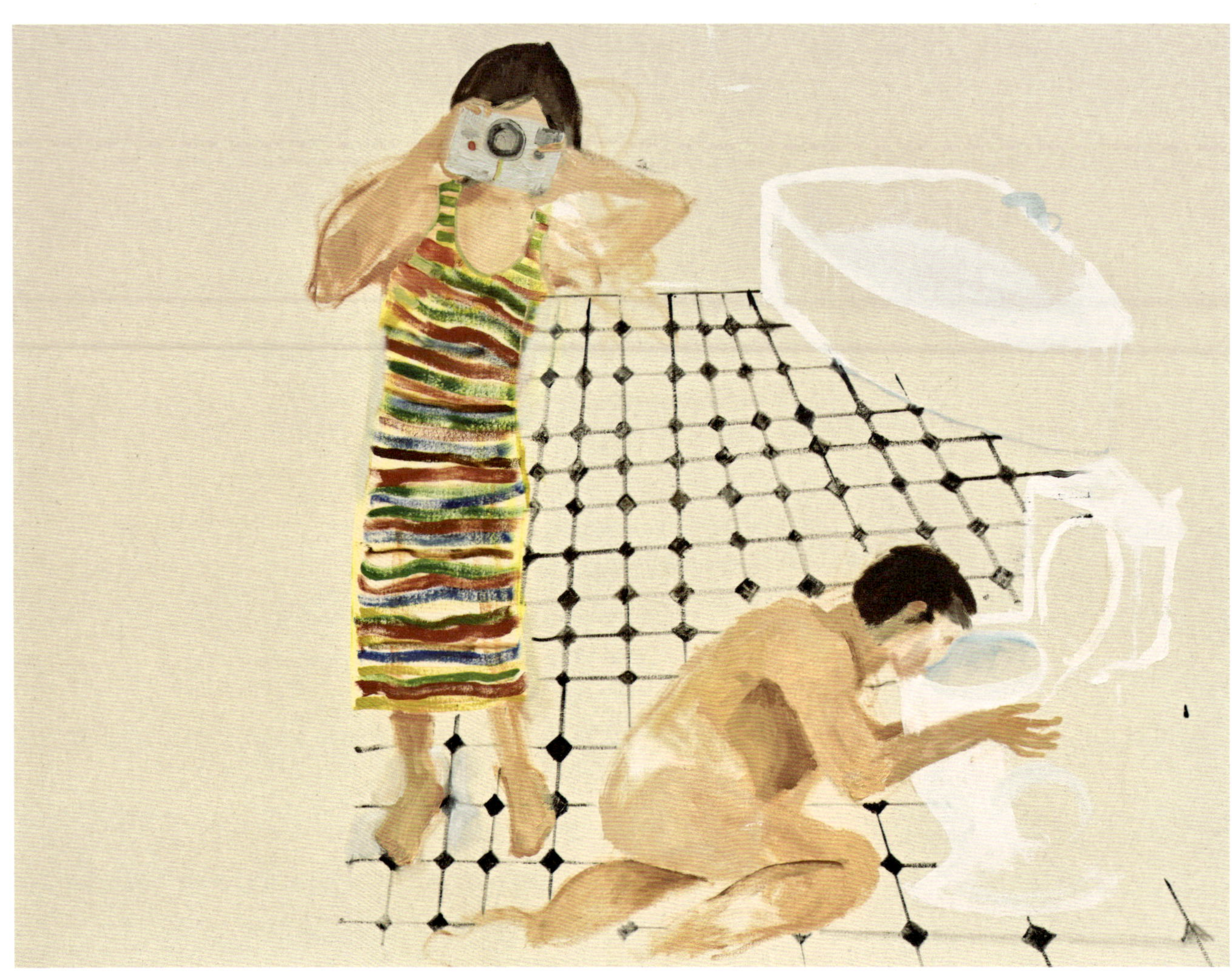

Lawyer
2022

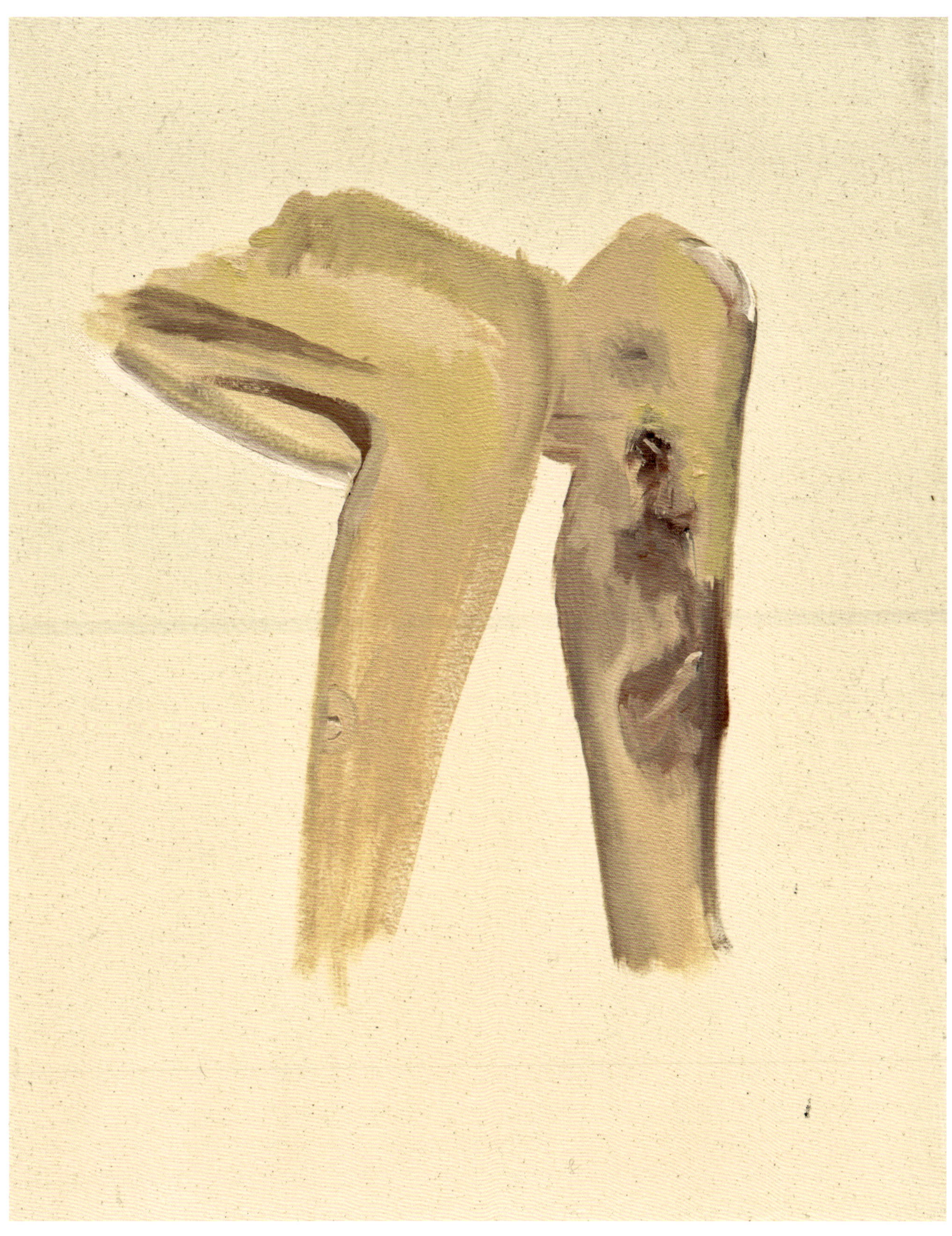

Legs
2022

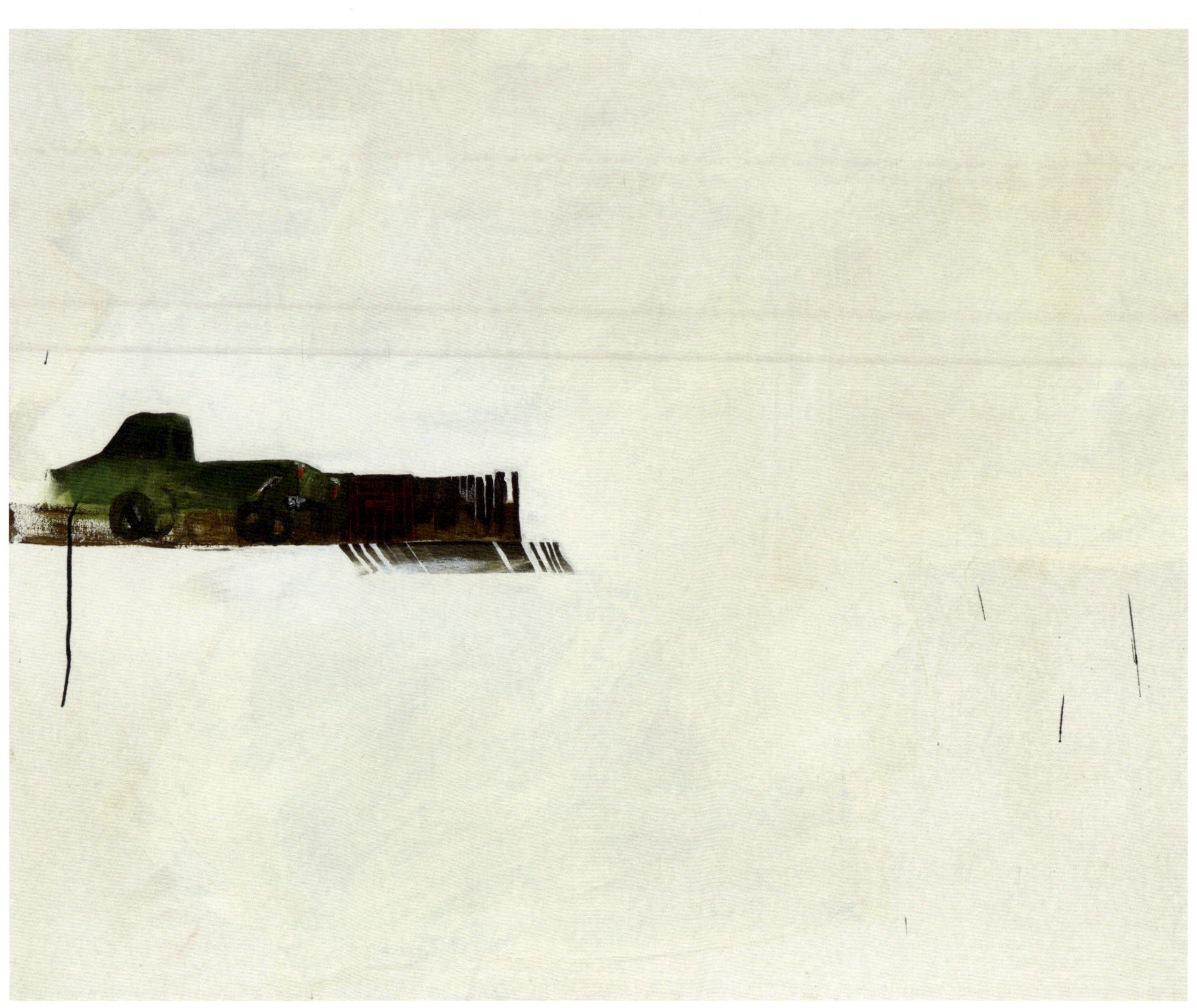

Flood
2009

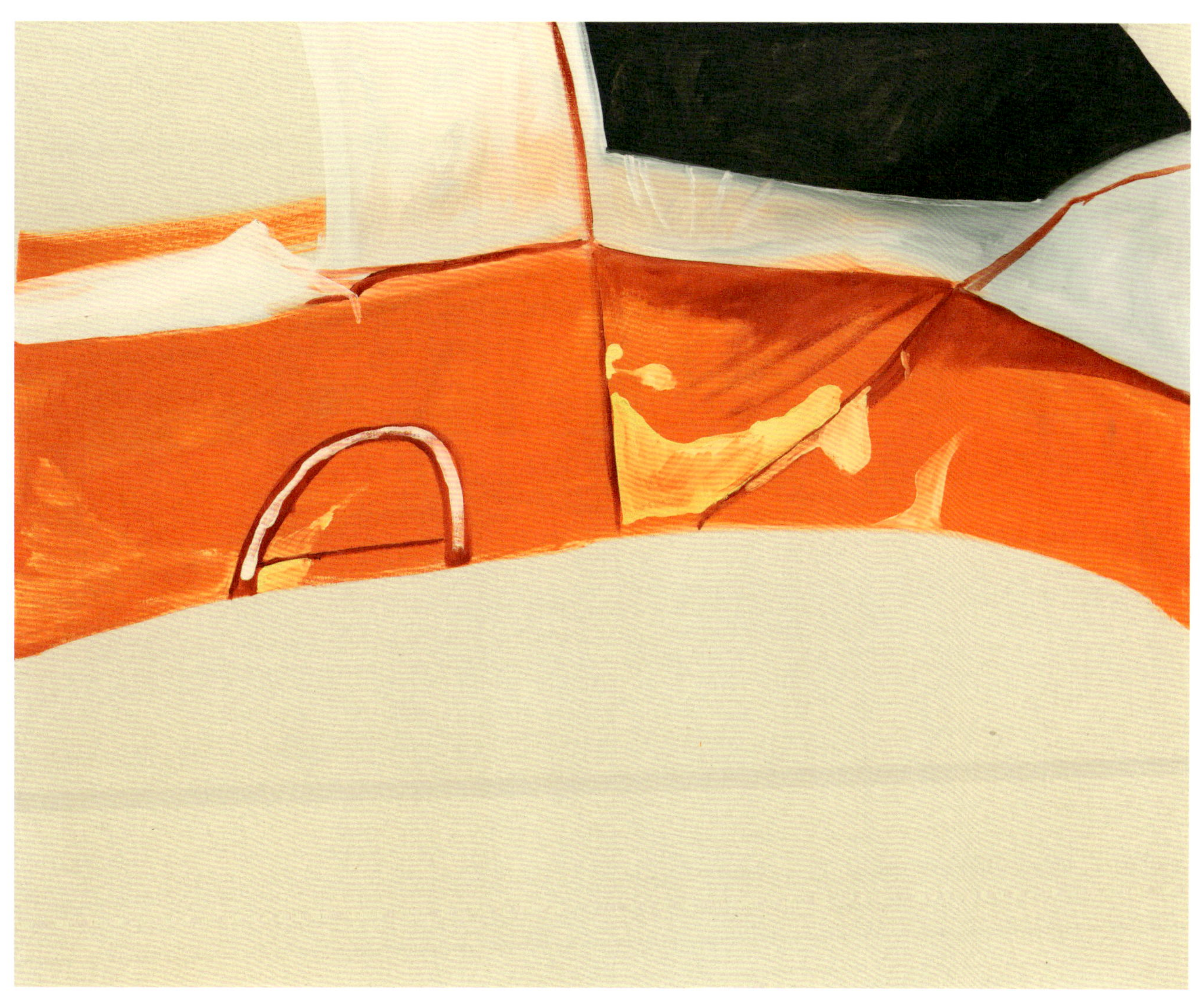

Orange Tent
2020

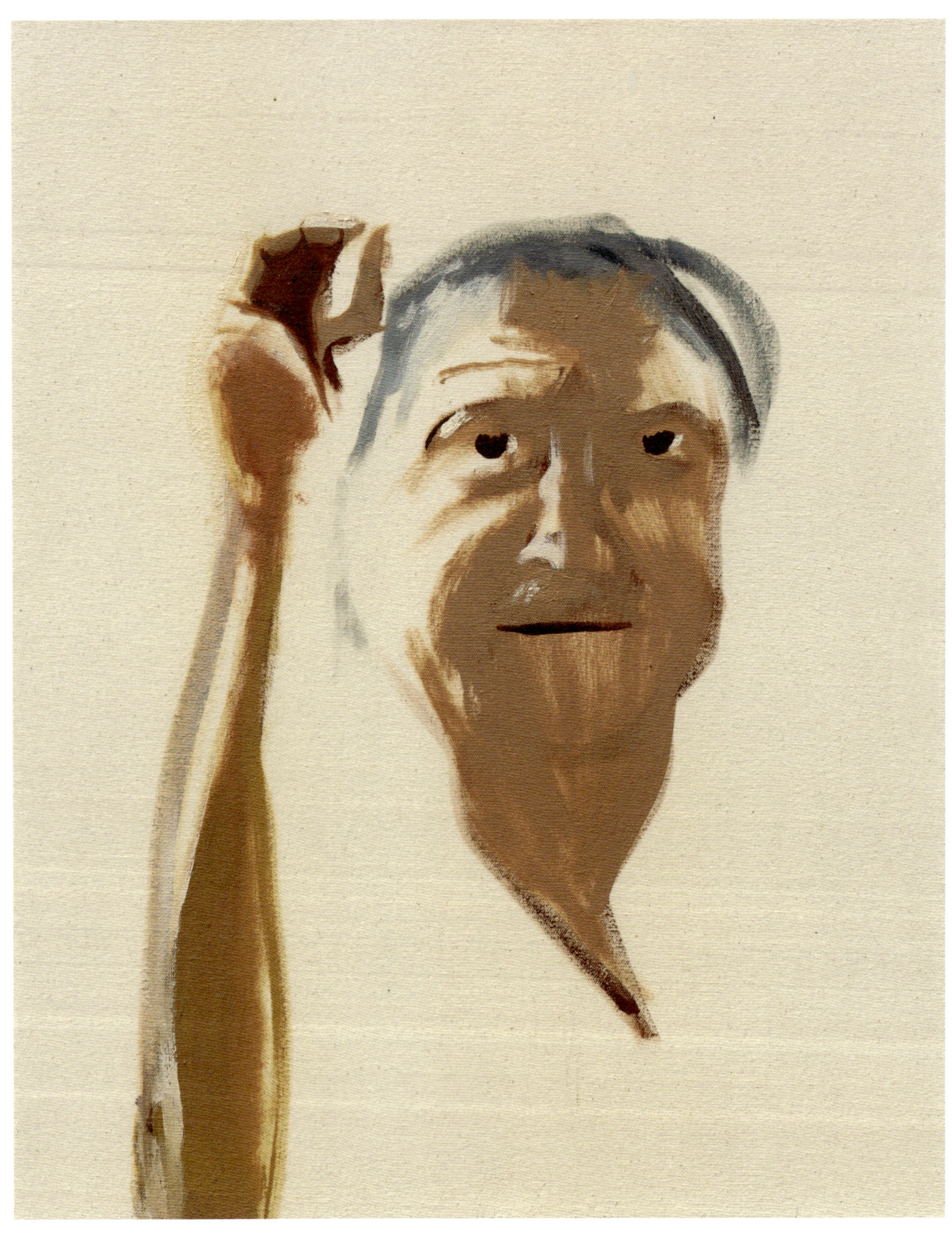

Pray
2020

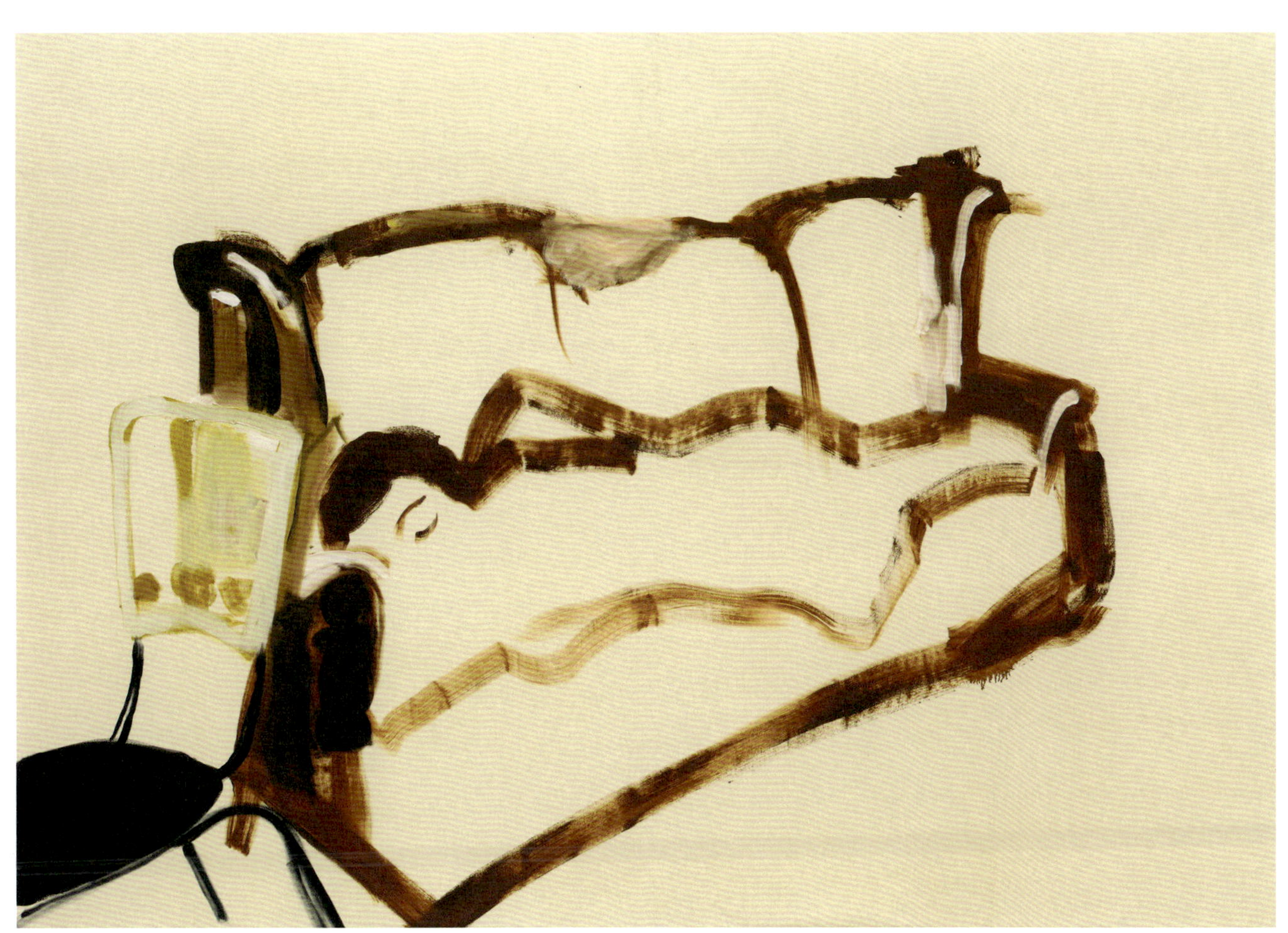

Rest
2021

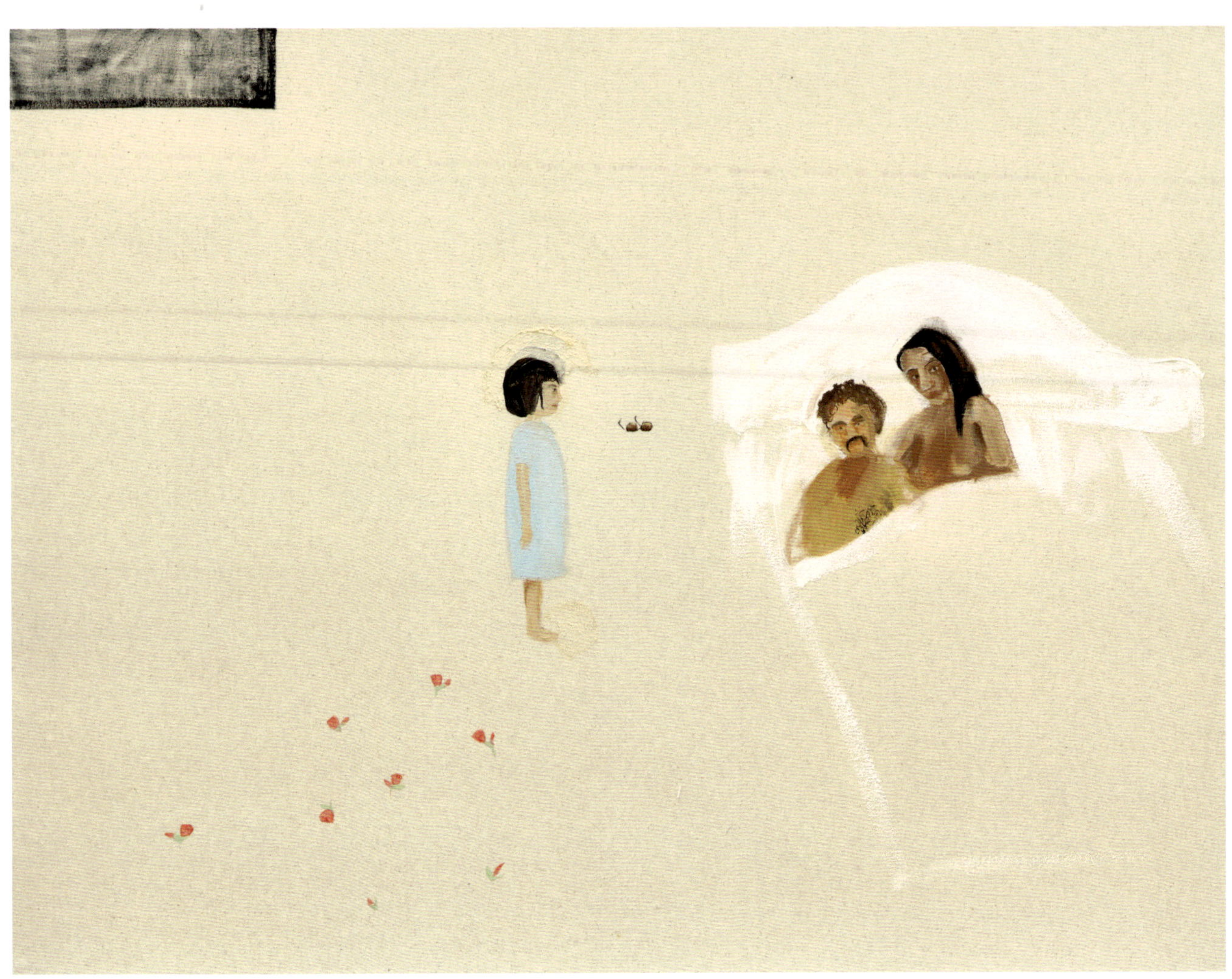

Rose
2019

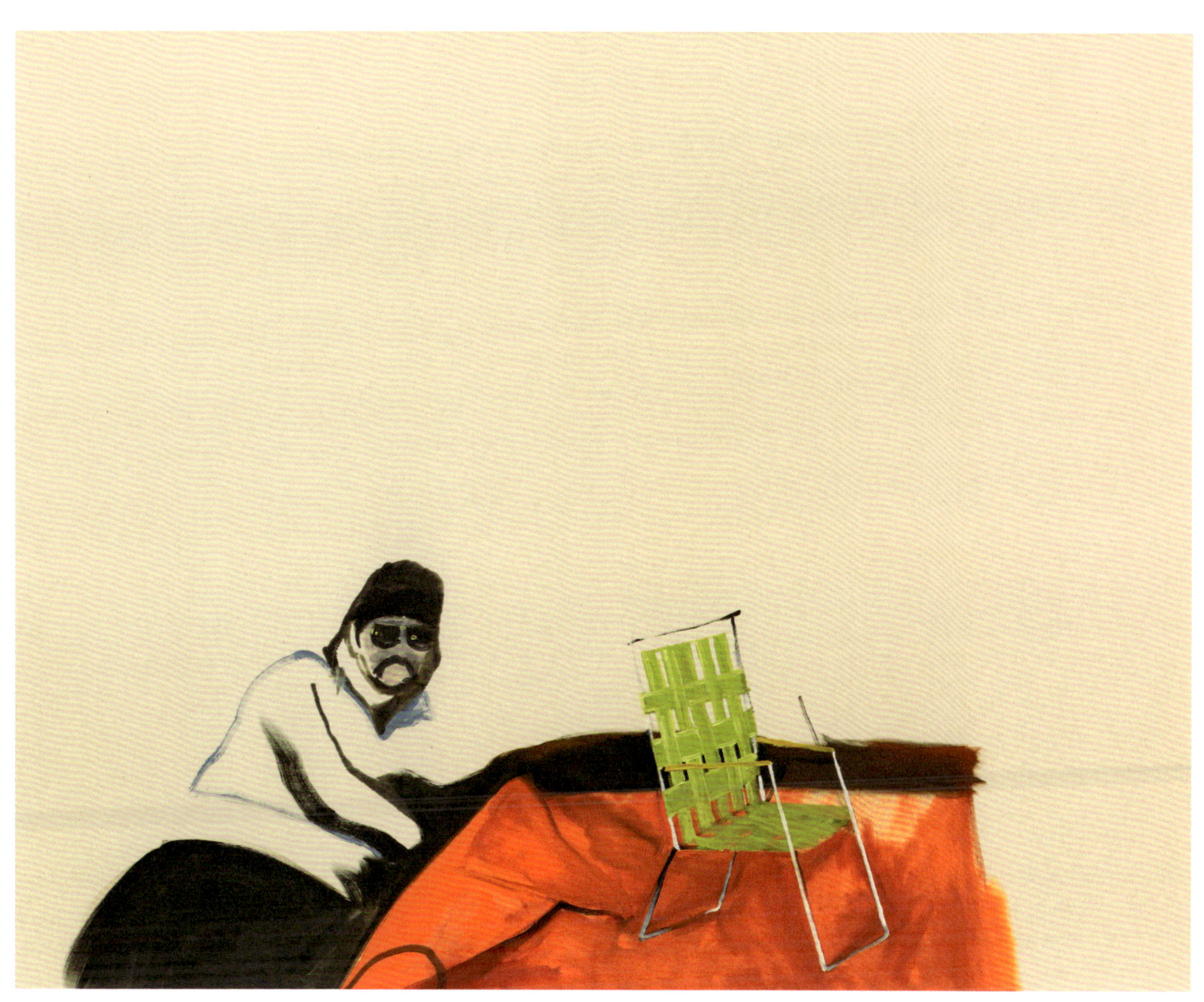

Strange Invitation
2020

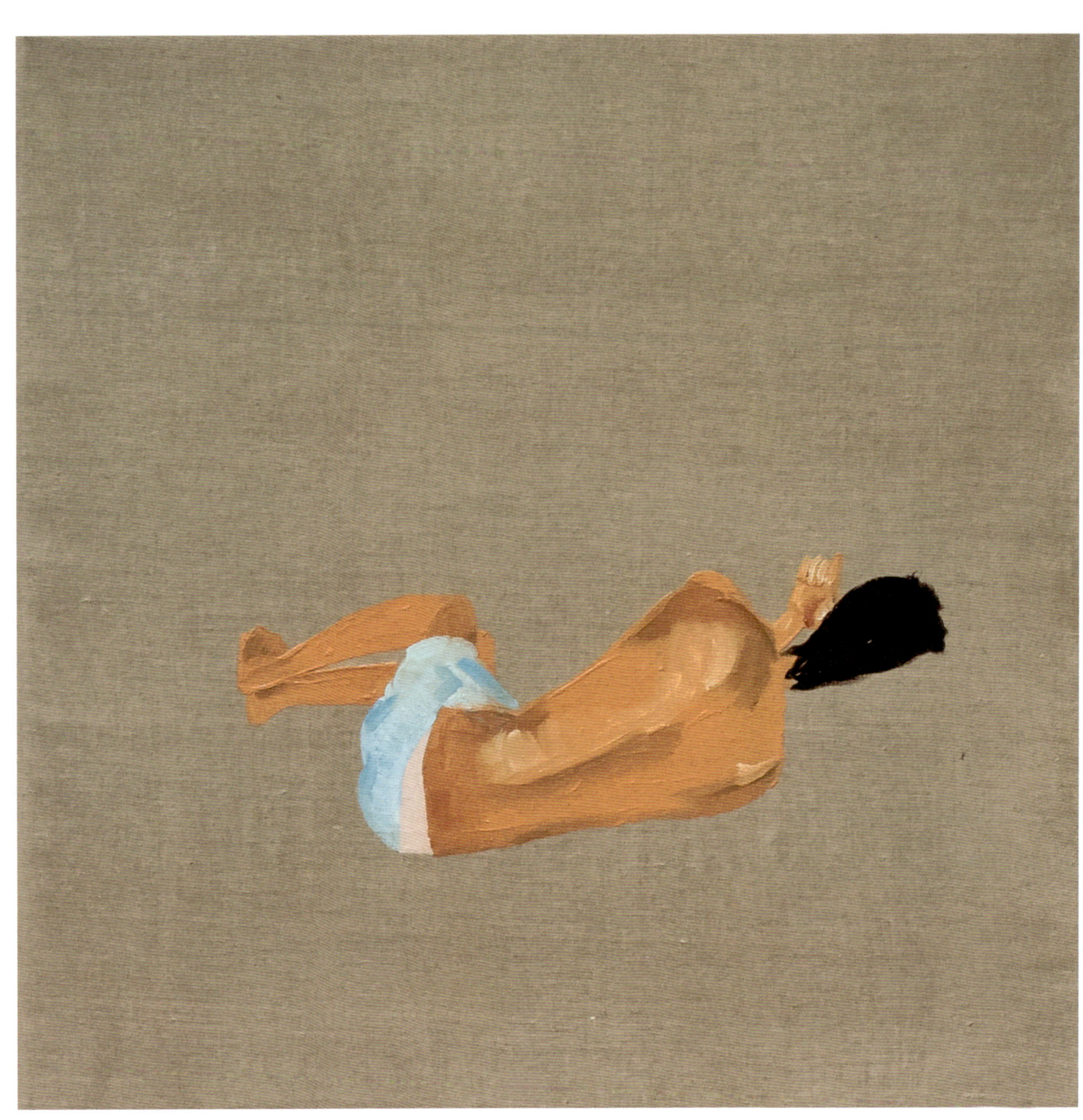

Summer Nap
2017

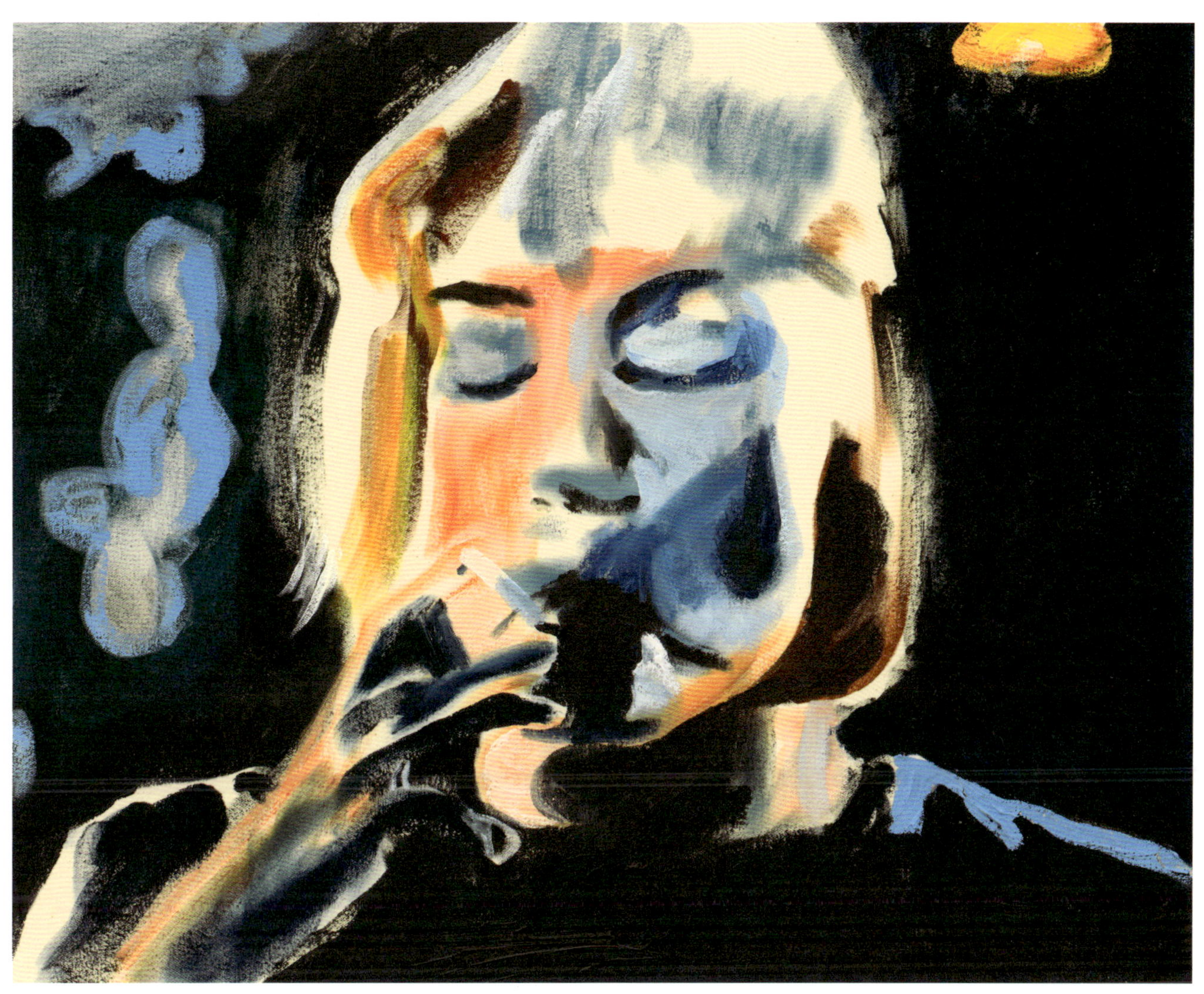

Teenager
2019

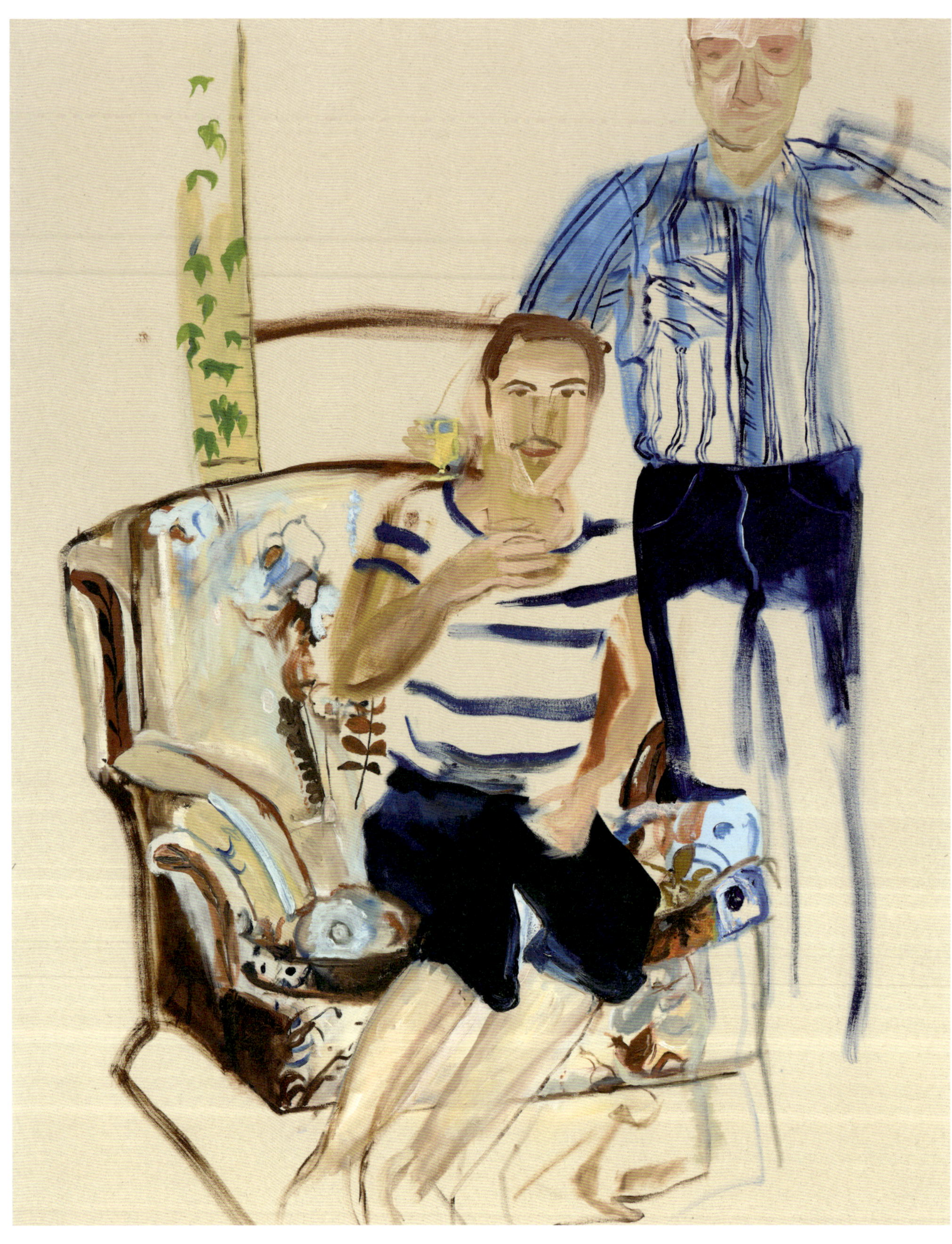

Toast
2022

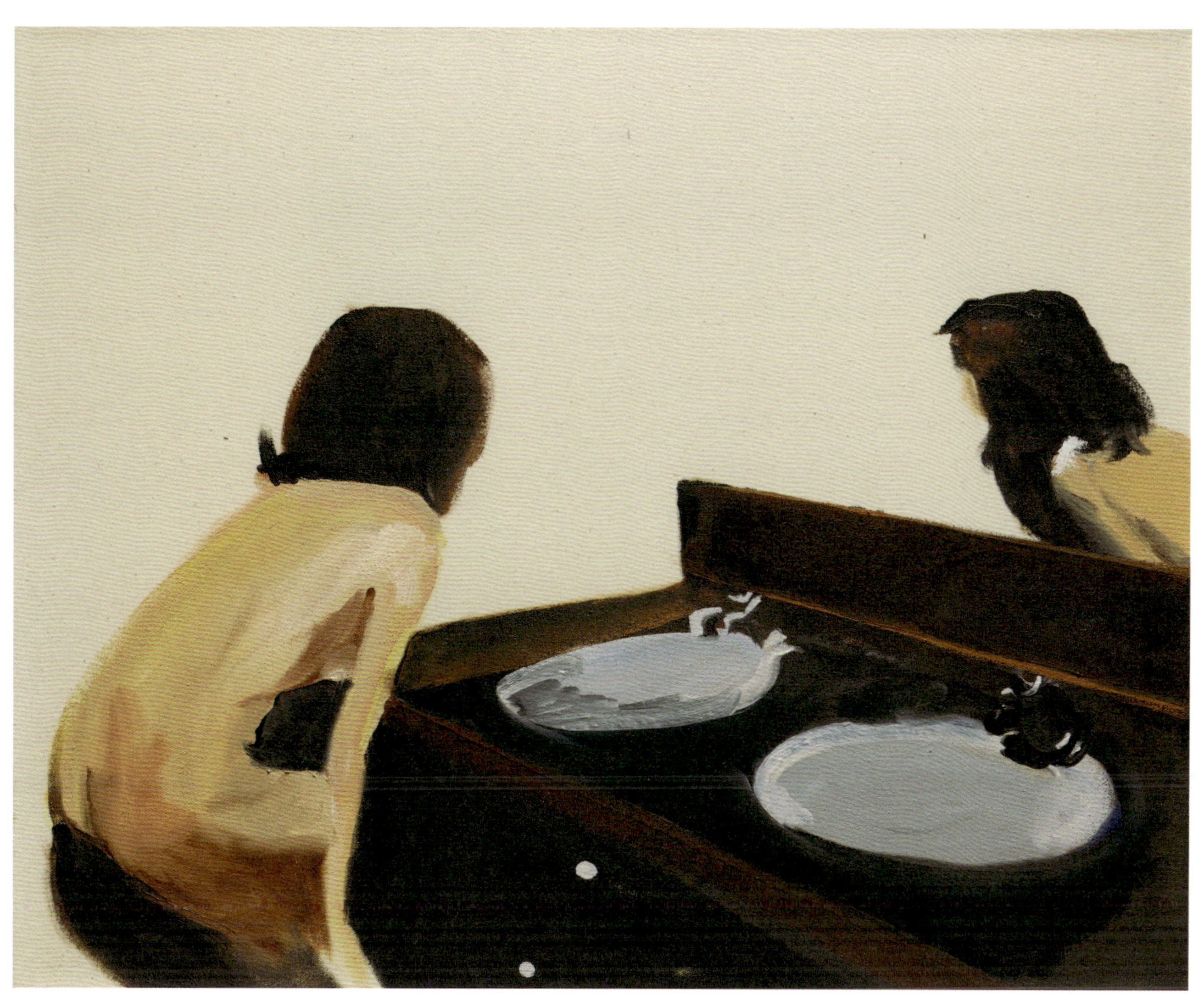

Vanity
2019

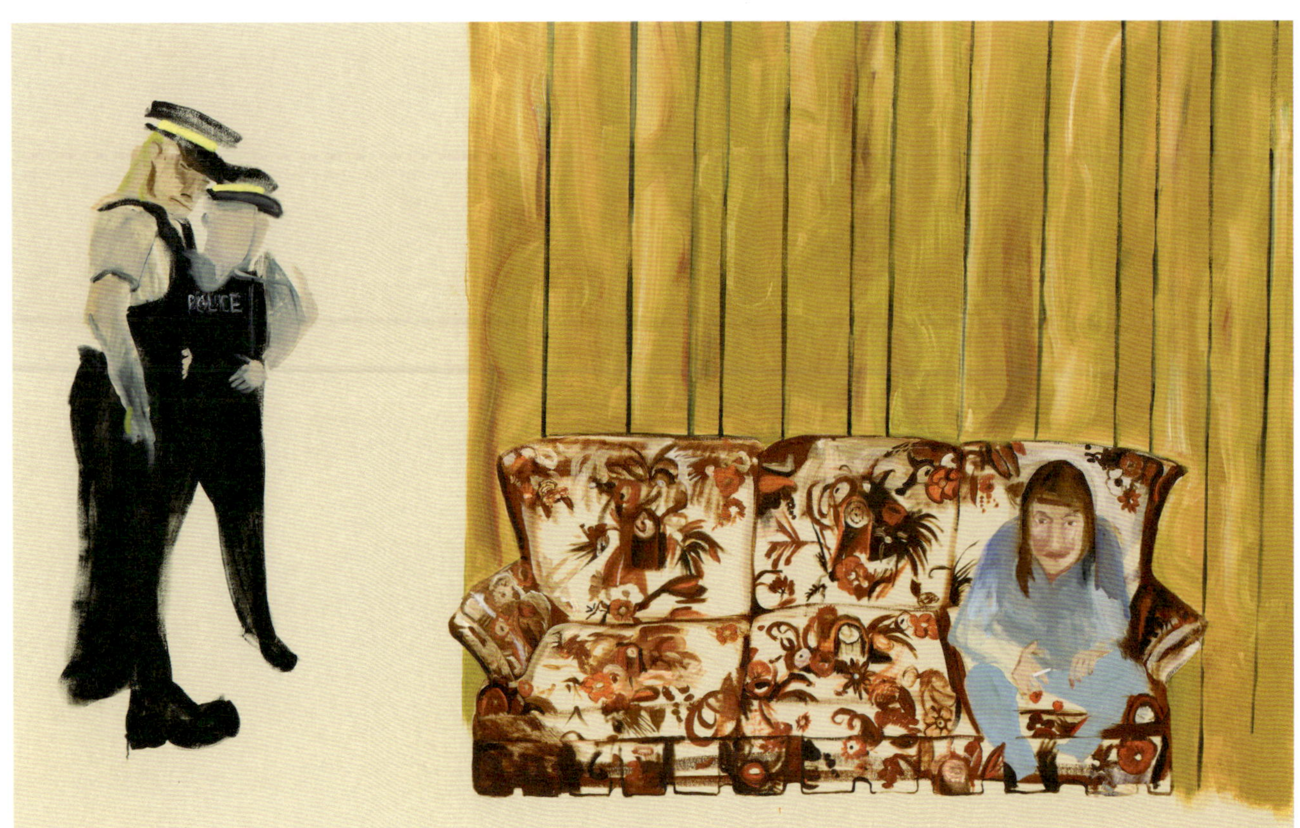

Visit
2021

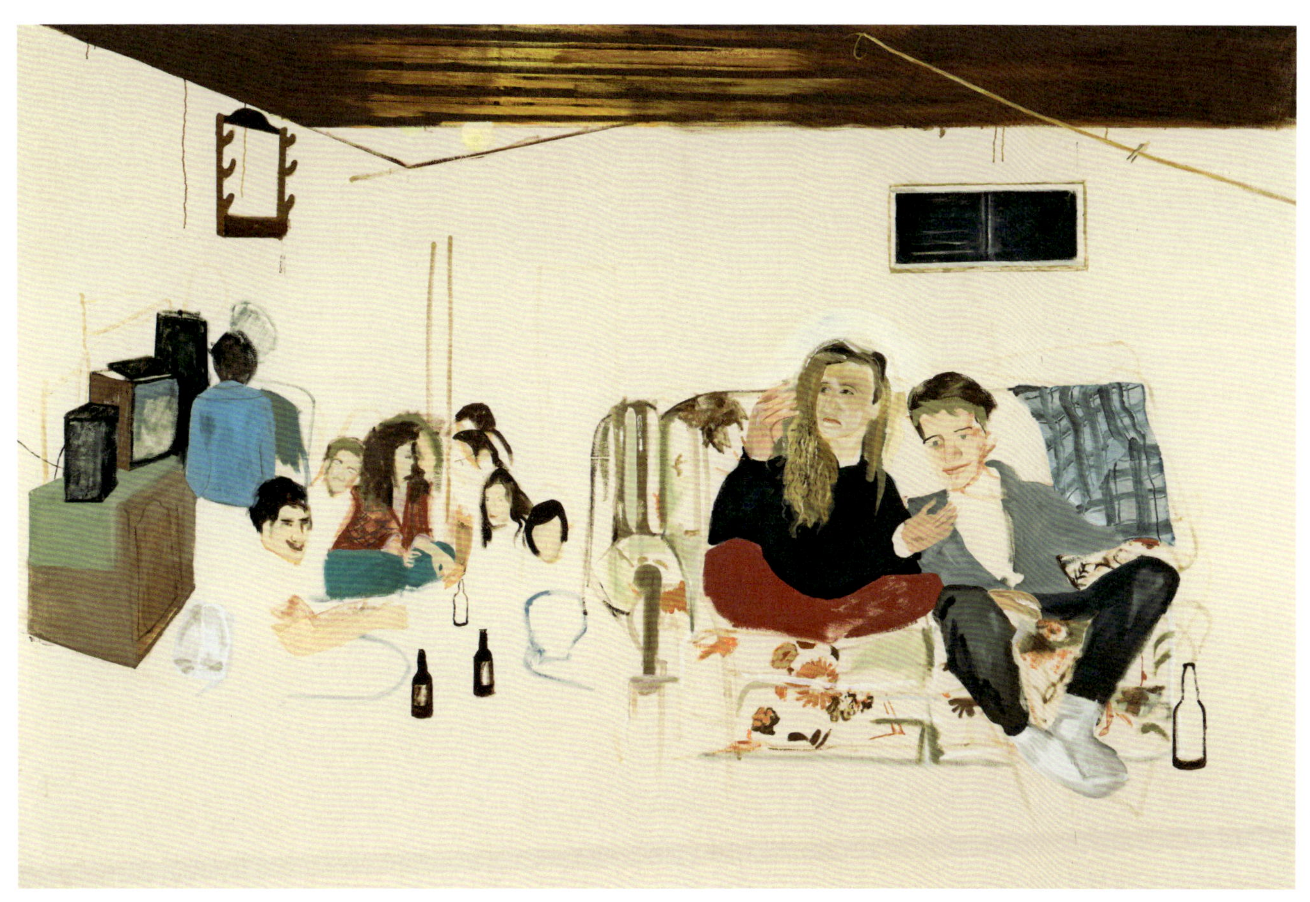

A Basement Party
2022

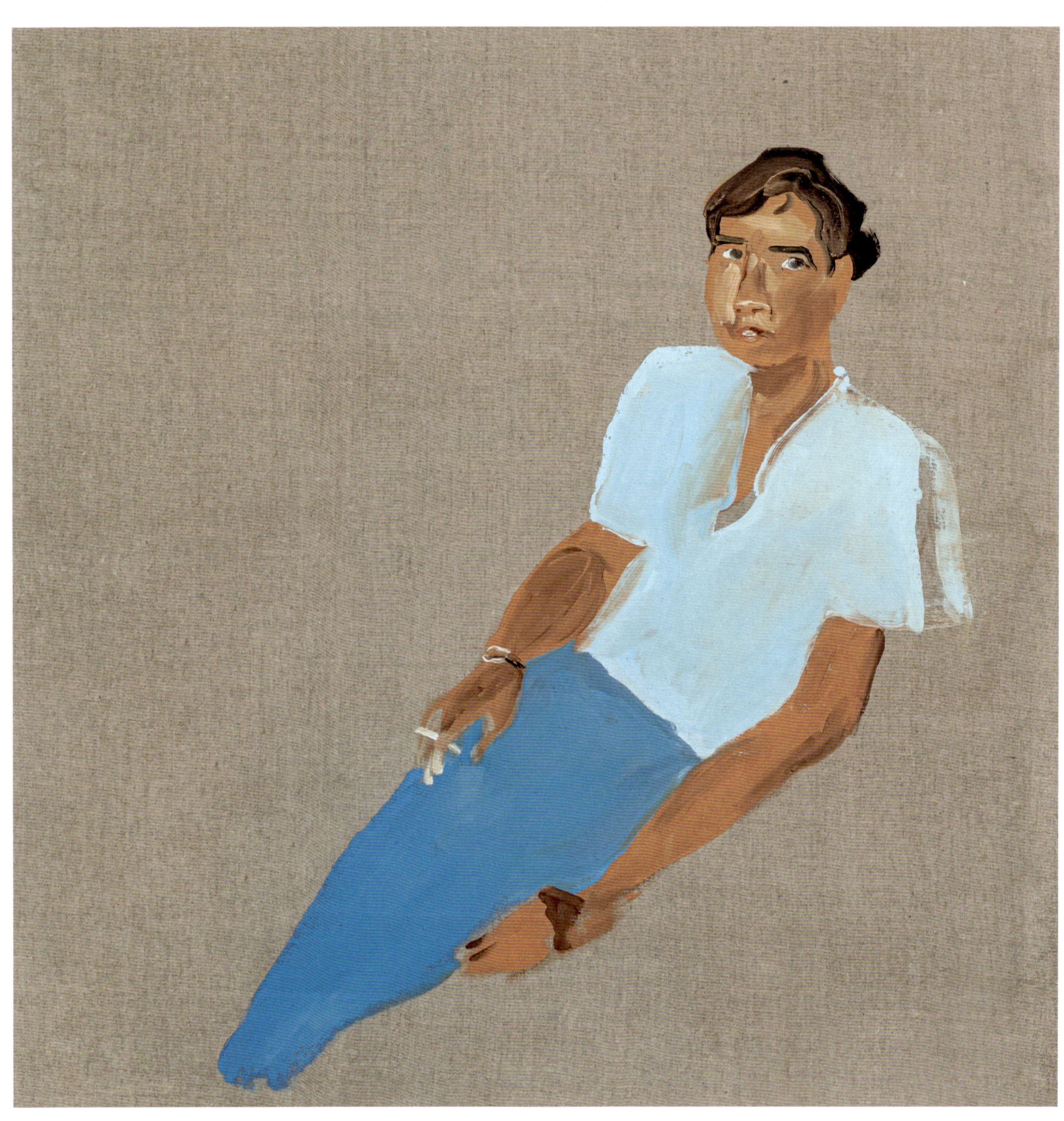

Dart
2017

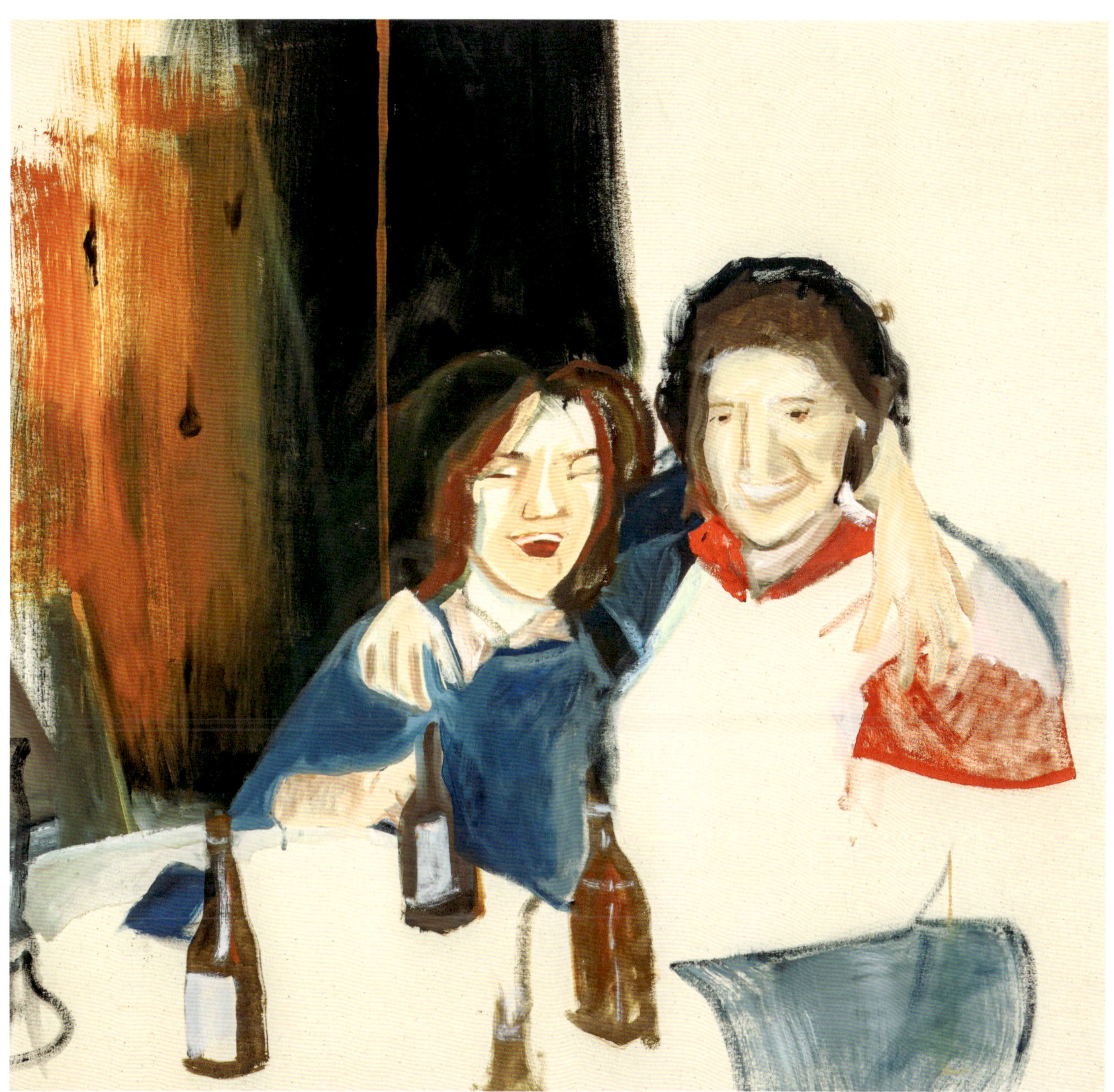

Diane
2022

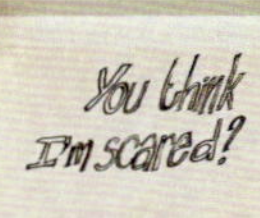
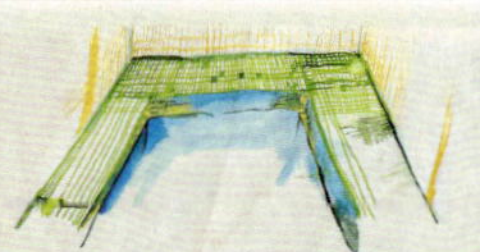

Scroll One
2010–ongoing

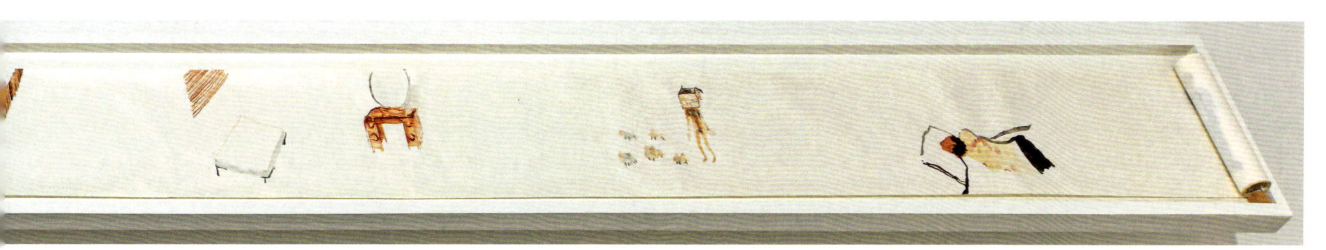

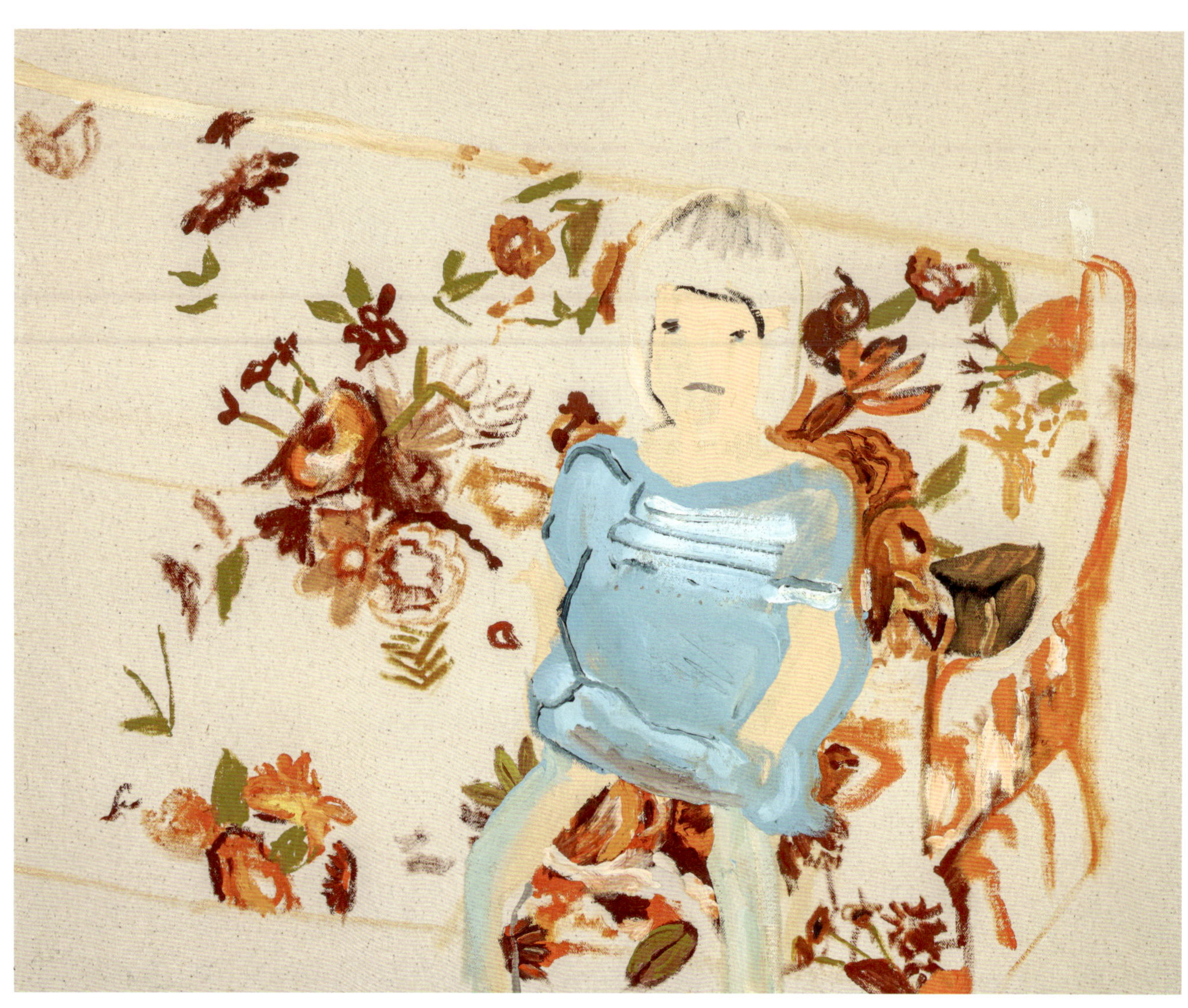

Self-portrait
2022

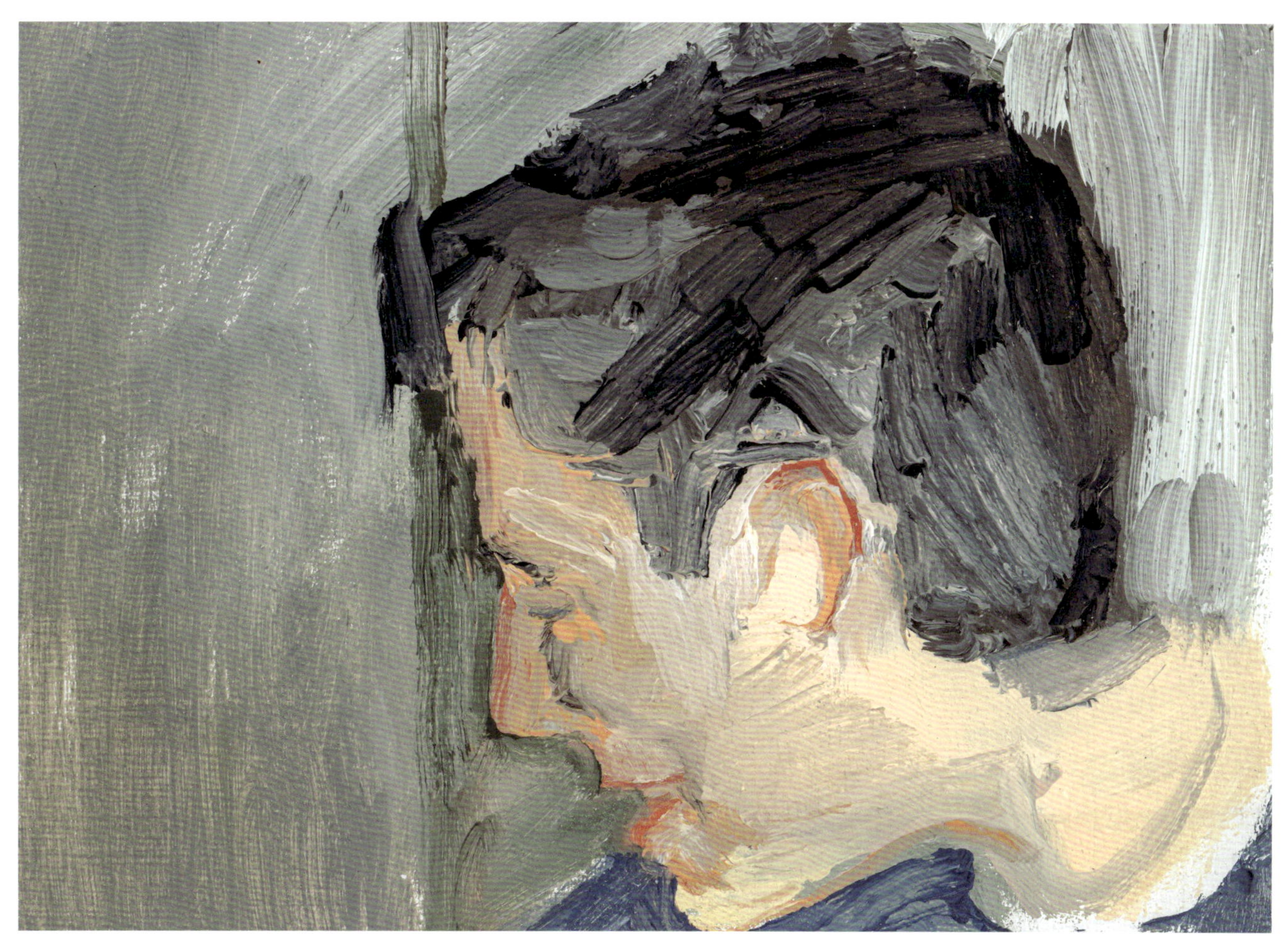

Shan
2013

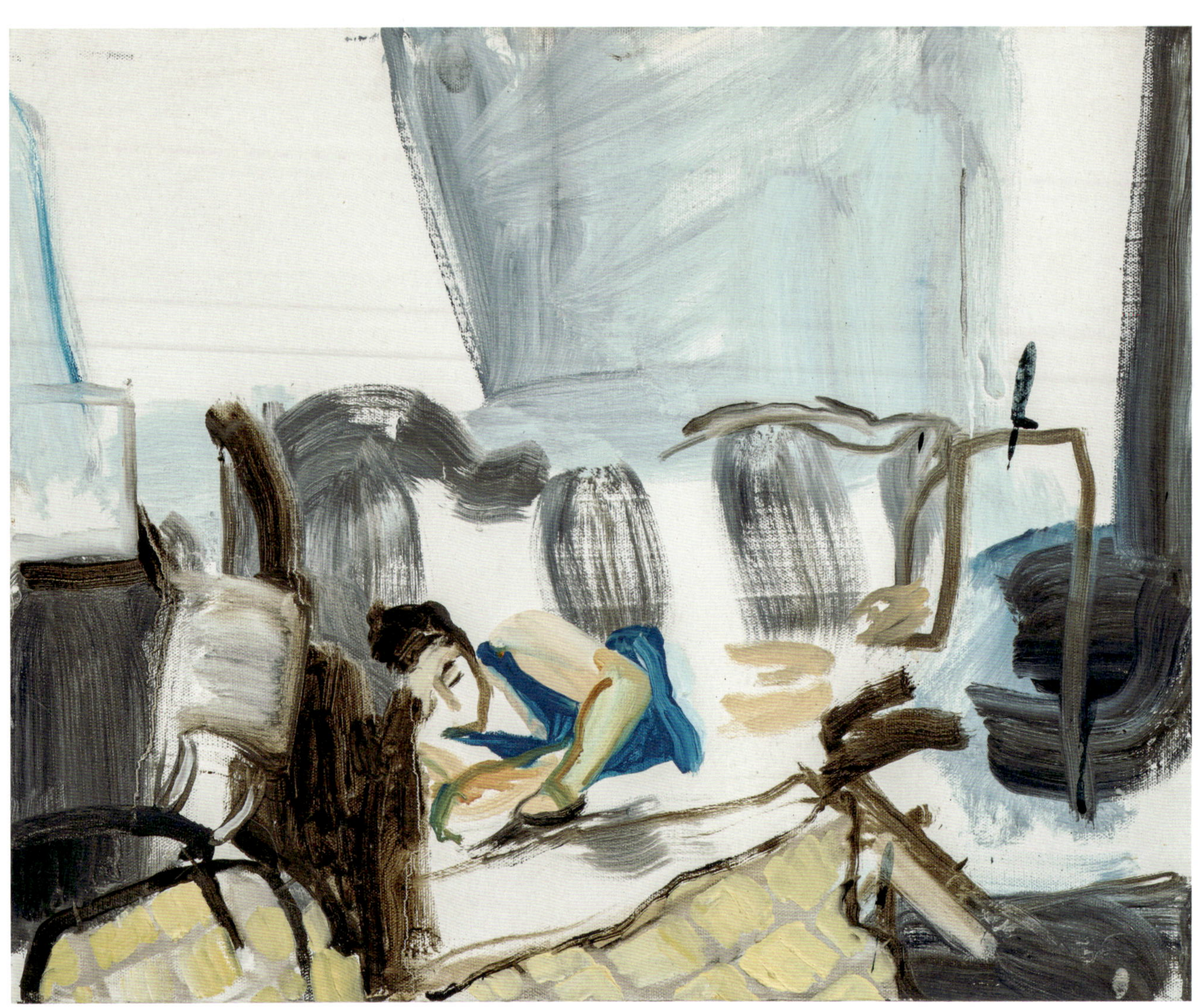

Sleep
2008

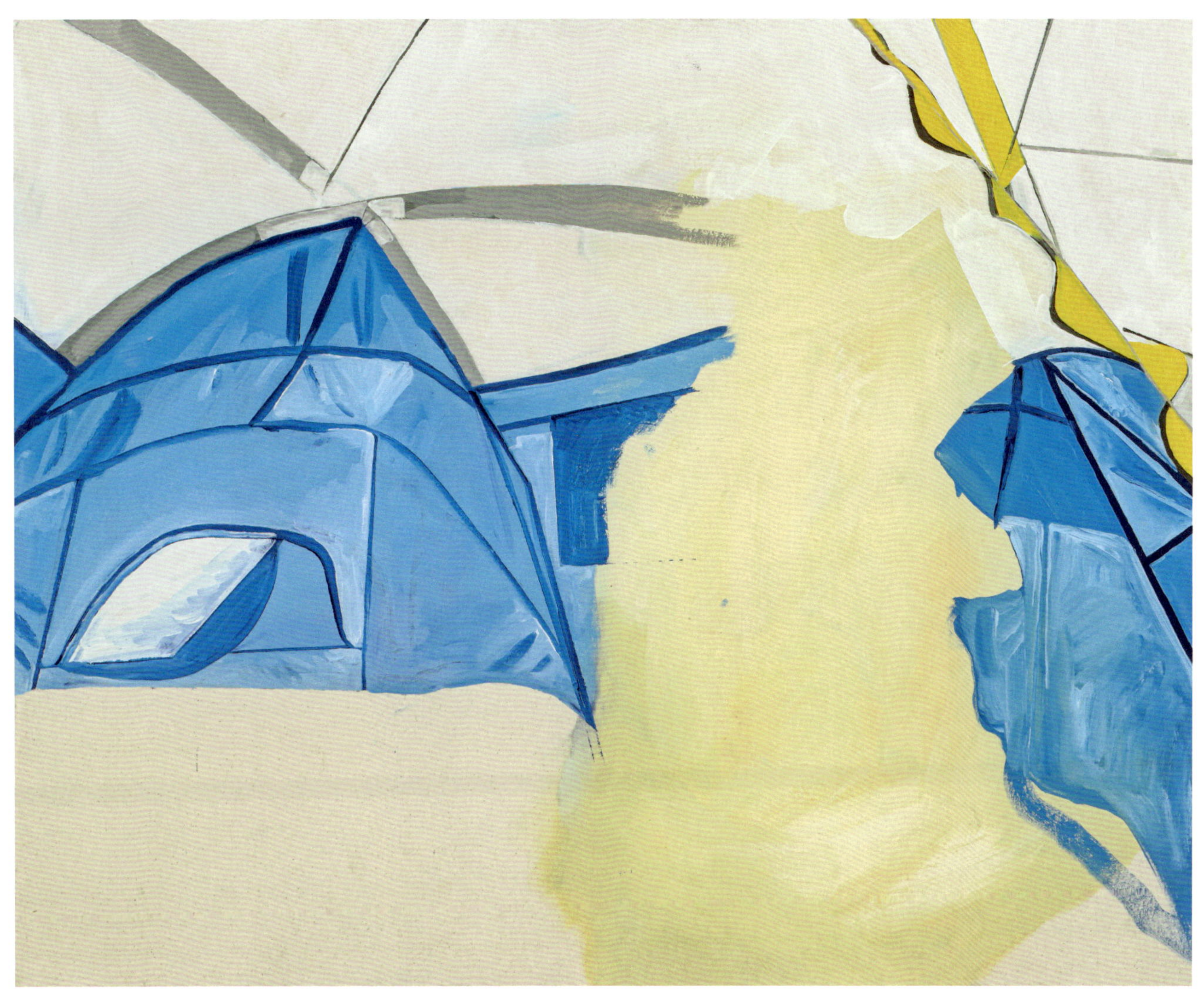

Tent City
2010

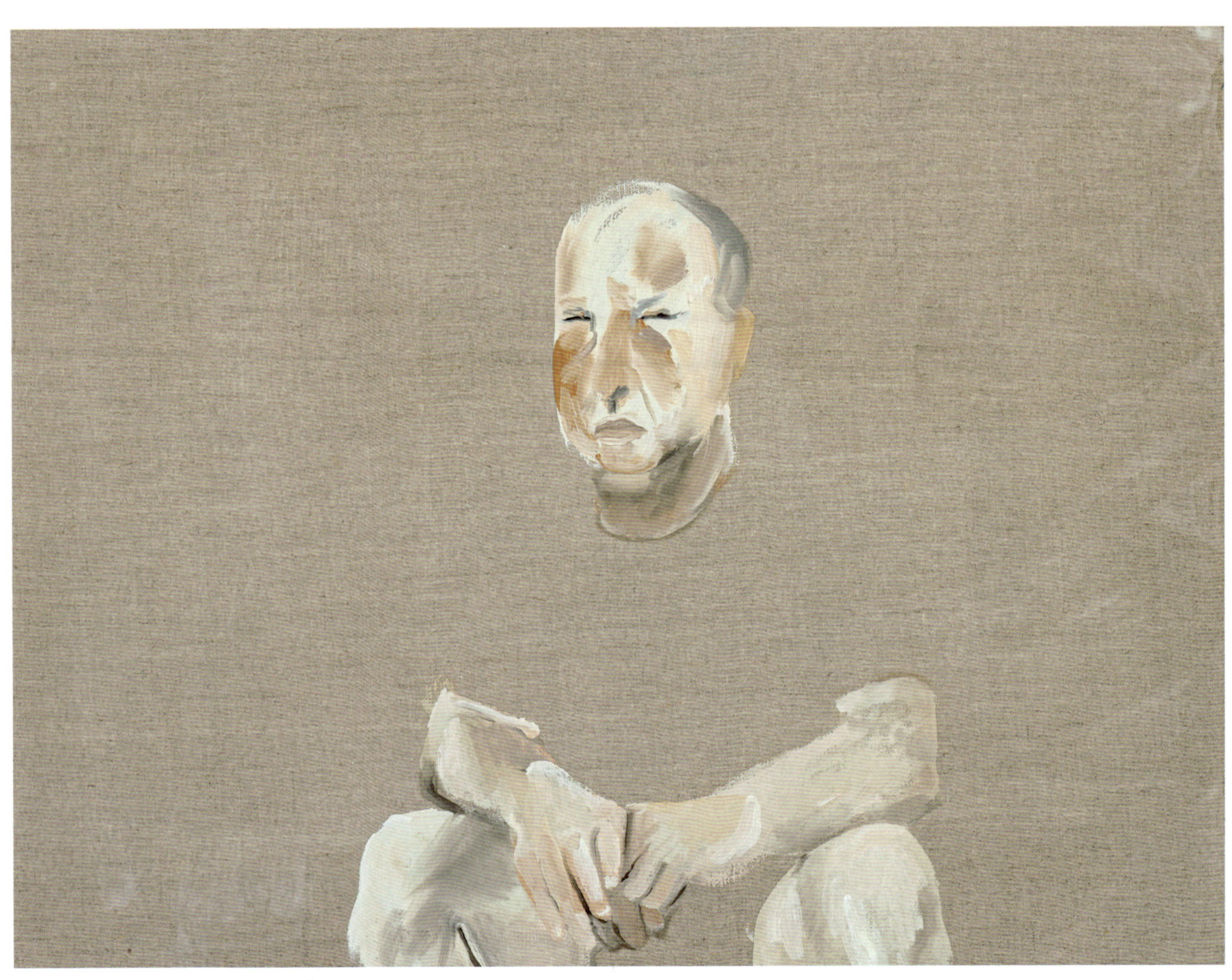

The Righteous
2010

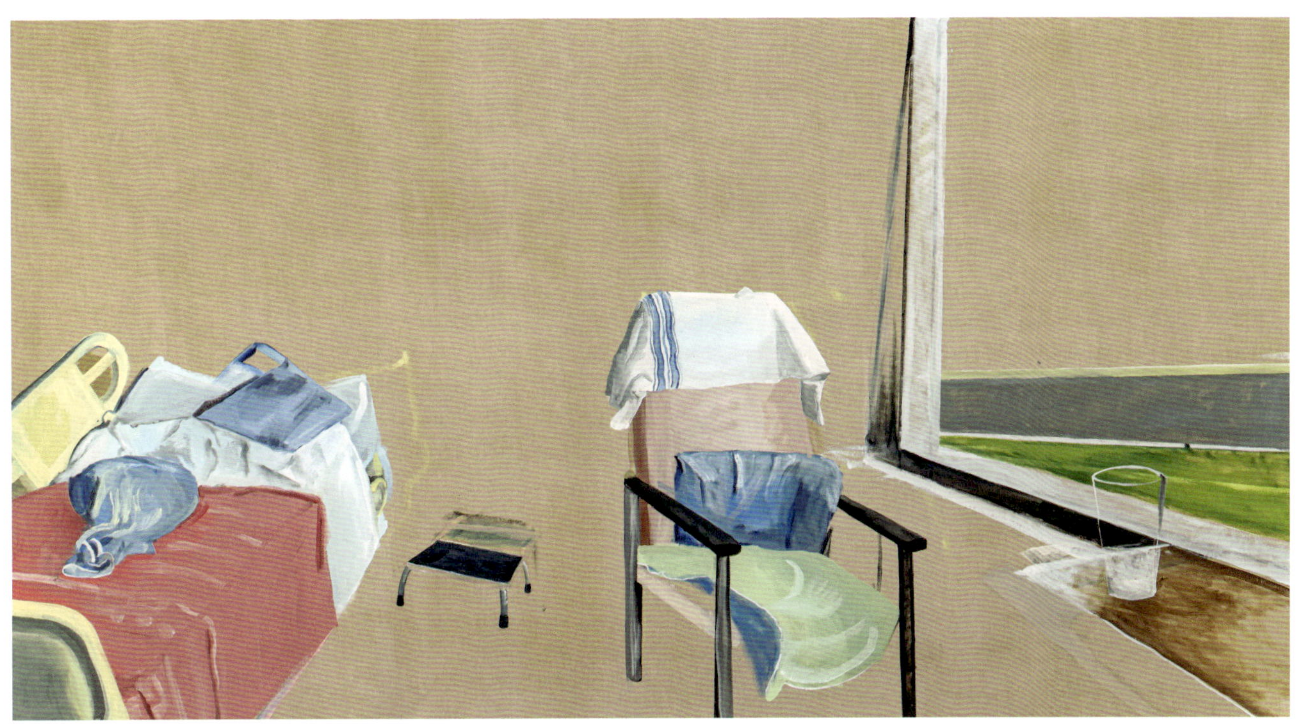

Theatre
2019

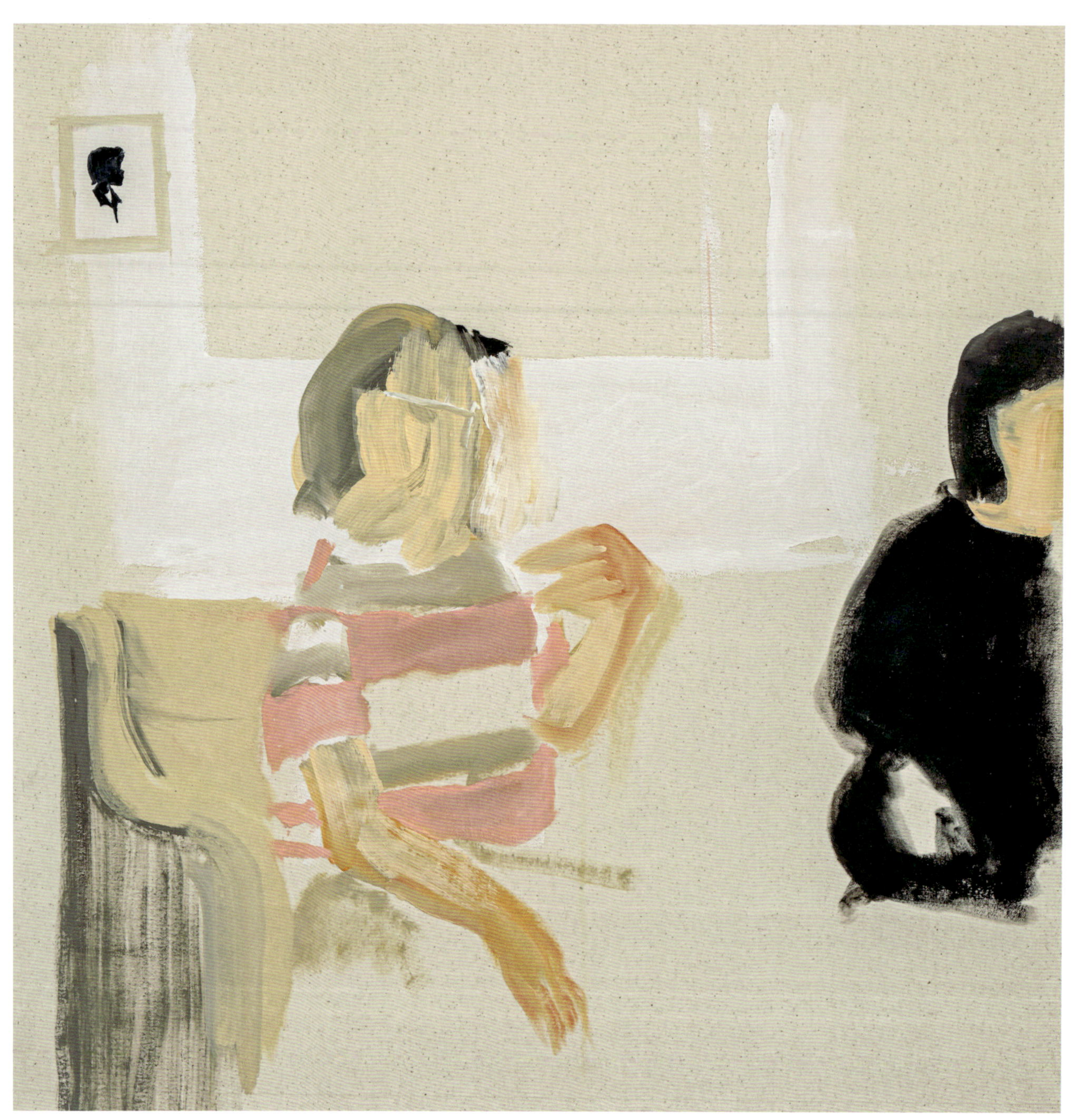

Women
2017

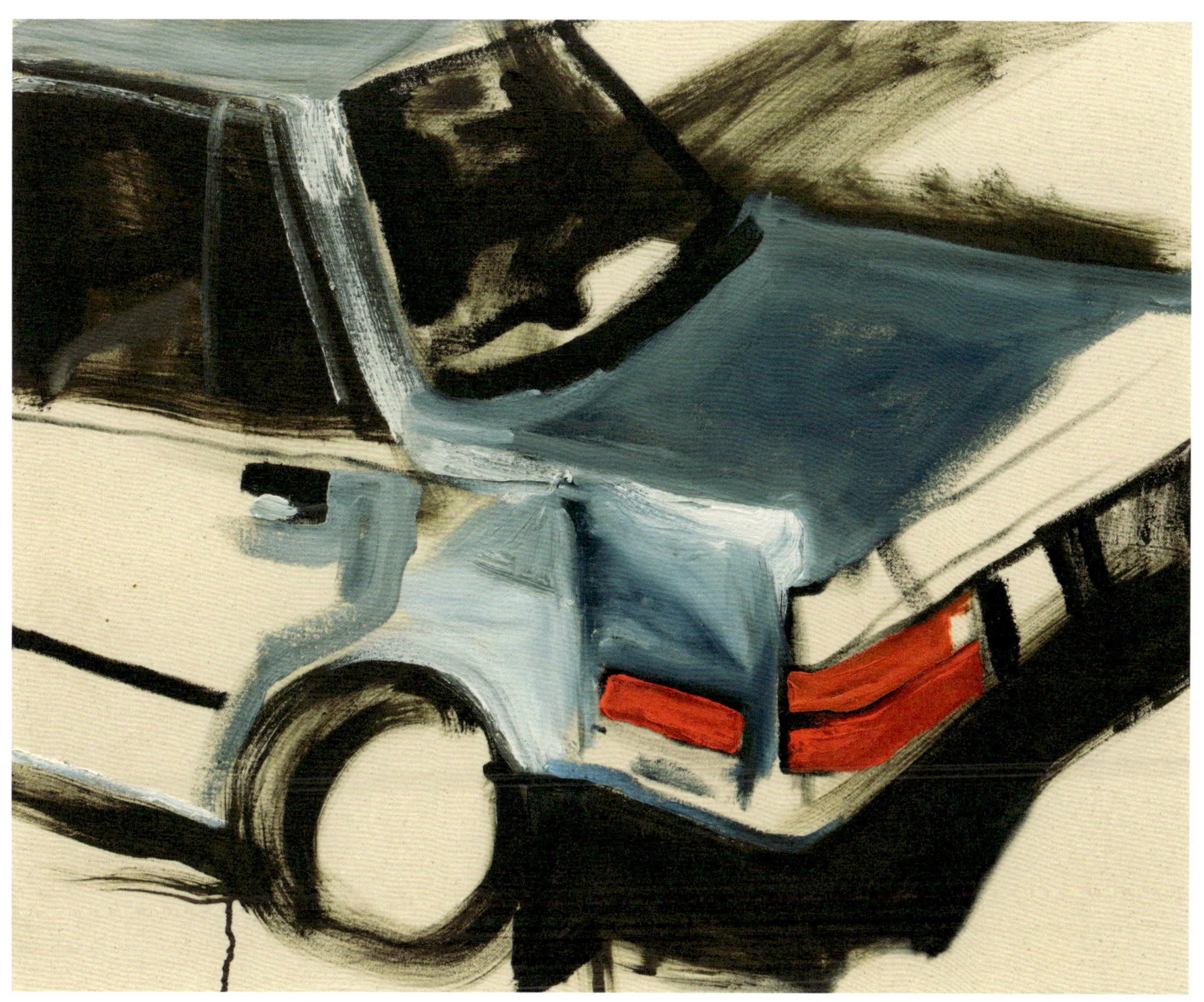

Accord
2021

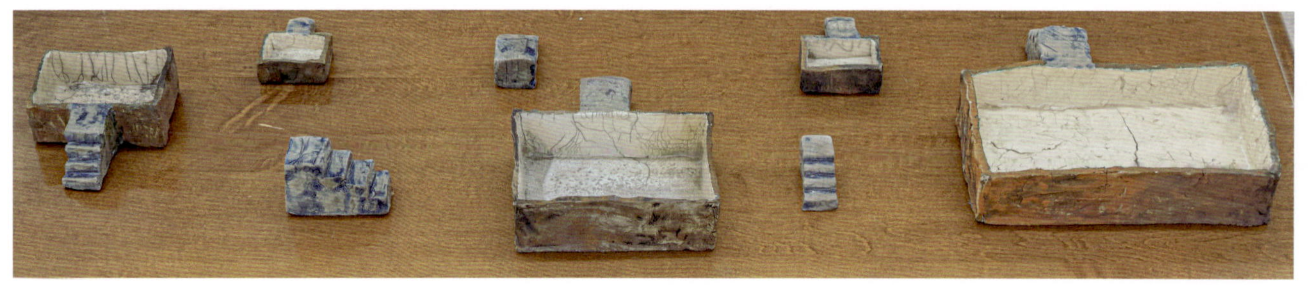

Parish 1–8
2010

BRENDA DRANEY: DRINK FROM THE RIVER
Jacqueline Kok

*A product of its time. This is all a product of the times.
Look at the sunlight, they say. How it falls right through. Some
things are hidden in plain sight. Look, there was so much
space back then. And you do look.*[1]
—Ocean Vuong, "The Punctum"

Engaging with Brenda Draney's paintings means exercising stillness.
It means venturing into a stillness so profound that it can leave
you unmoored from the social anchors that tether you to the daily
operations of modern life. It is a stillness that can be acute to
the point where it marks you, bequeathing a permanent scar deep
within the memories of your muscles. It is a stillness that, quite
frankly, scares me. It frightens me because, on the one hand, it
requires a willingness to be vulnerable and connect back to the most
intimate part of myself—the part hidden in the chasms of my
mind. On the other hand, it petrifies me because it allows my belief
systems to be challenged.

The stillness that I am referring to, however, is not one that
advocates for total inner tranquility, reminding us to relinquish
intrusive thoughts to bring full attention back onto a single point.
Rather, I am alluding to the kind of stillness that is closely related
to mindfulness and empathy, whereby the individual leans into their
feelings to activate introspective reflection. As such, it is the kind
of stillness that, ironically, prompts us to be unstill before achieving
any clarity regarding our sense of being or existence in the world.
Draney's paintings do not simply necessitate this kind of intense engagement; they are depictions that embody this experience as well.

At first glance, one could claim that there is not much to
be seen in Draney's paintings—only a setting of the stage, so to
speak. Yet, the emptiness stirs thought. And in continuing to
use theatre as the analogy, upon engaging with the works, we are
prompted to wonder what happens next, who the other actors
are, and how many other details have been left out. In fact, what is
presented to us is not spectacular in the Aristotelian sense—there
are no costumes, gestures, sounds, or visual effects.[2] When care-
fully observing the paintings, it becomes clear that Draney makes
intentional decisions concerning what remains unseen. This careful
dance between absence and presence—of questioning the minutia
of the image—that appears on the canvas is also the juncture
where vulnerability lives.

Take *Accord*, 2021 (see p. 67), for instance. In painting the
rear profile of a Honda Accord, Draney has presented the essentials
of the scene. Anything outside of this depiction remains undeter-
mined. What makes this composition, as well as Draney's other works,
compelling is that she chooses something familiar: a car lauded for
its affordability, reliability, and functionality, making it one of the
best-selling and most recognizable automobiles in the world. However, the untouched spaces in the painting invite each viewer to
share their own associations with the vehicle. A fill-in-the-blank, if

1 Excerpt from *TIME IS A MOTHER* by Ocean Vuong, copyright © 2022 by Ocean Vuong. Used by permission of Penguin Press, an imprint of Penguin Publishing Group, a division of Penguin Random House LLC. All rights reserved.

2 Spectacle, according to Aristotle, is one of the six components that comprise a tragedy. To the philosopher, spectacle is the least important, as a tragedy's delivery can be independent of such elements. It can even be argued that Draney purposefully does away with the spectacle, with superficial embellishments that serve to awe rather than to authentically capture the action depicted. See: S. H. Butcher, *The Poetics of Aristotle* (London: Macmillan and Co. Limited, 1902), 22–31.

3 Brené Brown, "Places We Go When Things Don't Go as Planned," in *Atlas of the Heart: Mapping Meaningful Connection and the Language of Human Experience* (New York: Random House, 2021), 38–55.

4 In his book *The Body Keeps Score*, US-based psychiatrist Dr. Bessel van der Kolk explains that people who have experienced trauma tend to have fragmented or even forgotten memories of the incident. Yet when confronted with similar elements from the moment (i.e., images, sounds, and physical sensations), individuals respond as if they are living in the moment again, despite being able to conscientiously draw the connection to the past event. See Bessel van der Kolk, "Part Four: The Imprint of Trauma," in *The Body Keeps Score: Brain, Mind, and Body in the Healing of Trauma* (New York: Penguin Books, 2014), 171–201.

you will. But beyond that, the depiction can also be beguiling, encouraging viewers to take these connected moments and memories and go one step further: the Accord, simply put, is not considered a luxury car. With this in mind, we might begin to wonder what other kinds of deeper—maybe even contentious—observations, judgments, or stereotypes can be evoked. Absence and stillness, then, can dredge up suppressed, forgotten, and awkward feelings. However, as American professor and author Brené Brown teaches us, "Sometimes the most uncomfortable learning is the most powerful."[3]

When conscientiously thinking through these recollections that surface while we engage with Draney's paintings, we also become subsequently tasked with parcelling and piecing these memories, determining which ones have truly metamorphosed over time. Furthermore, once someone else's take on that moment is added to the mix, the truthfulness of the memory is challenged. Whose version is the accurate one? What other specificities have slipped through the cracks? We endeavour to remember events with meticulous precision because we hope that they can provide answers and alleviate any sense of anxiety related to something long forgotten or even shamefully buried away. Some would even audaciously try to recreate a past event, believing that its presence will reveal truths. Yet those who hold on unyieldingly to the past are left with sorrow upon realizing that nothing can ever truly be perfectly revived. Paradoxically, for those who insist on being relieved of a haunting memory, they are betrayed by their bodies, which respond almost automatically to similar, painful events.

This tension—the piercing experience from the intense desire, knowing that we are neither able to recall our past with extreme precision nor able to turn back the hands of time, whether it be to undo or redo something—is no better encapsulated than in *Shan*, 2013 (see p. 55), which depicts the profile view of a figure who is seemingly looking away. The flatness of the subject and the room conveys a kind of compression of time-as-depth—we are in the present, now and always, no matter how much we yearn for the past. Eyes blurred and lips agape and pulled back ever so slightly, the figure is frozen mid-sentence—perhaps even mid-thought—looking back, figuratively and metaphorically speaking. Alternatively, this condensing of time can feel abrupt and disorienting. For example, those suffering from trauma may experience their body reacting before their mind does when triggered, activating the various components of the brain, including the amygdala, which is responsible for the fight-or-flight response. The body memorizes trauma even when the brain forgets.[4]

What does it mean, then, to radically accept vulnerability or to lean into the emotions that make us feel naked and unarmed? To answer this, it is important to emphasize how *avoidance* of stillness is antithetical to unstillness. Avoidance can be understood as purposefully not showing up to the things that feel all-consuming. It results from and harvests more anxiety. In jolting, testing, and questioning our memories through the blank spaces in her canvases, Draney asks us to walk together with stillness so that we may unearth meaning from within ourselves to create connections with those around us. Not only is this in itself a prompt to exercise empathy, but it is also a glimpse of the Real.[5] Draney creates works that capture the troubling and unsettling fragments of life that we normally filter out or are unable to apprehend head-on in her paintings, all of which are borne from references to her lived experiences and the critical moments from the community to which she belongs. To be unstilled by Draney's paintings, then, can be seen as a willingness to courageously sit at the edge of uncomfortable knowledge, to again quote Brené Brown, alongside the artist.

We also see this engagement in *Legs*, 2022 (see p. 21), a painting of an unknown person's shins. The right leg is severely bruised, the blue and purple hues having blossomed into distinct patches against the fair-skinned limb. Who these legs belong to and how exactly they were injured is, for the most part, irrelevant. What we end up observing is a moment frozen in time, the consequence of an injury that came to light after the fact, and evidence that something indeed happened, even though we have no record of it. This depiction puts into stark focus the wound itself—a memorialization of sustained damage inflicted on the body. Put another way, bruises form when small veins and capillaries break, creating a pool of blood outside the blood vessel but always underneath the skin. The manifestation of the physical trauma remains partial. Such devoted attention to this common blue-and-purple mark makes us think deeply about the precarious relationship we have with bodies, particularly our own. What is visible versus hidden?

This ambivalence of being neither here nor there, of stillness and unstillness, of absence and presence—which was brought up at the beginning of this text—conjures up the concept of the trace developed by Algerian-born French philosopher Jacques Derrida (1930–2004). Trace is one of Derrida's core concepts that reacts against the idea of meaning being stable or the idea of words coinciding fully with themselves. For Derrida, words—and other signifying units—make sense by pointing elsewhere, by referring to that which they exclude or are not: "the retention of difference within a structure of reference where difference appears *as such* and thus permits a certain liberty of variations among the full terms."[6] In other words, the trace refers to the empty presence of a word, which contains its opposing meanings via their absence. Truth, then, is elusive, as meaning-making is a circular and even subjective and vulnerable process. Yet to access signification we need language. Viewed through this lens, the parallels between Derrida's trace and Draney's paintings can be made: trace as a condition of any form of signification exists in the artist's unique visual language, always alerting us to their opposites; breaking down claims to ultimate truth; and highlighting the absences that are otherwise overlooked.

Nevertheless, to equate Draney's paintings to a narrative, even her own, would only misguide us, as doing so would limit the scope of her works. Similarly, trying to find a common denominator, like a shared or relatable experience, may bring us closer to Draney's depicted subject matter, but it would still inadequately capture the

5 I am specifically referring to the Real in the Lacanian sense. French psychoanalyst and psychiatrist Jacques Lacan (1901–1981) described the Real as one of three structures that make up the psyche, with the Real being the state of human nature that encompasses the whole material reality outside of the self and is thus too traumatic to be encountered fully. In Lacan's words, the Real is "either totality or the vanished instant." Severed from us once we have accessed language that provides structure and order, the Real is often described as "impossible" precisely because it cannot be written or spoken. Whereby reality is constructed by way of accepting the rules around linguistic expression and therefore the social norms—the Symbolic—to cope with unfulfilled (egotistical) desires—the Imaginary—the Real correlates in opposition to both the Symbolic and the Imaginary to undermine such reality and reveal, for lack of a better word, the essence of our existence. See Jacques Lacan, "The Symbolic, the Imaginary, and the Real," in *On the Names-of-the-Father*, trans. Bruce Fink (Cambridge: Polity Press, 2013), 1–52.

6 Jacques Derrida, "Linguistics and Grammatology," in *Of Grammatology*, trans. Gayatri Chakravorty Spivak (Maryland: Johns Hopkins University Press, 1997), 27–73.

7 Lisa Hix, "It Came From the '70s: The Story of Your Grandma's Weird Couch," Collectors Weekly, August 27, 2018, https://www.collectorsweekly.com/articles/it-came-from-the-70s-the-story-of-your- grandmas-weird-couch/comment-page-1/.

8 Roland Barthes, "Studium and Punctum," in *Camera Lucida: Reflections on Photography*, trans. Richard Howard (New York: Hill and Wang, 1982), 25–27.

nature of the subject matter—its essence as well as the various interconnected ideas and facts that comprise it. For example, the couch featured in some of Draney's paintings, such as *Visit* (see p. 42) and *Rest* (see p. 29), both from 2021, illustrates the importance of stepping away from overarching symbolic meanings (like couches representing family time) and instead seeks the generative powers of these depictions. The floral-patterned upholstery of Draney's couch, in fact, is a direct descendant of Colonial Revival—a style that yearned for the aesthetics of America's founding period. Ironically, though this period's traumatic history has cast a dark shadow and legacy on the ways in which communities have been formed, classified, and (mis)treated, this flower pattern had a surge in popularity between 1950 and 1980, making its way into countless homeowners' living rooms.[7]

With this context in mind, we might begin to pose specific questions, as we did with *Accord*, related to notions of belonging and assimilation across generations and social strata, just to name a few. In *Self-portrait*, 2022 (see p. 52), we see a painting of the artist on the couch, yet the patterned upholstery slowly recedes, eventually disappearing altogether as our gaze edges toward the painting's frame. While the figure is a depiction of Draney herself, it can also stand in for any individual in the sense that the image prompts us to ask: How might her/my relationship with the couch impact world-building and meaning-making? And, indeed, as the couch in the painting fades toward the background, we, in turn, begin to respond by casting our own unique projections onto the blank spaces.

Once again, we find ourselves positioned in the liminal territory between the aforementioned dichotomies, both in our formal reading of Draney's paintings and in the affective sense. This endless choreography between the two polarities indicates that the loss of something, its complete absence, can birth new understandings. And, as previously mentioned, the strength in Draney's works lies in the distinctive relationship established between each viewer and each painting. It is akin to the concept of the punctum, the indescribable stinging sensation that emerges upon engaging with an image that exists independently of any cultural or social connotations, developed by French literary theorist and philosopher Roland Barthes (1915–1980).[8] These understandings are personal, irreplicable, and sometimes deeply painful. Through Brenda Draney's poignant depictions of life as (mis)remembered, we thus come to accept that memories, stories, and histories undergo changes, and new variations of the same old songs are made endlessly. But her works also suggest that rather than trying to find an origin story, our bigger purpose is to remain still as we embrace the possibility of loss and revel in the unstillness that succeeds in these shifting moments.

Brenda Draney is as careful and tentative with her words as she
is with her application of paint. She explains that her practice "has
something to do with narratives or stories."[1] Her paintings may
have "something to do with," but are not themselves, stories. If
they were, she might have made them more legible. Instead, they
are rough, sketchy, seemingly unfinished. They purposely resist
certain and easy "reading." If her brush strokes "speak," they do so
in whispers, mumbles, and melodies. While inspired by stories
and memories, Draney does not narrate or memorialize her subjects.
Rather, she raises doubts about whether such actions—narration
and memorialization—are possible or even desirable. Her practice
is less about the remembered than about the struggle to represent
the enigmatic phenomenon of remembering. Draney's non-linguistic
medium, paint, seems to have been chosen as a means to avoid
narrative capture, to show what a story can only describe. These
are self-conscious paintings: works that show their work. Incomplet-
ely smeared with oil and pigment, they do not disguise their nature
as stretched cloth rectangles. Uncertain, partial, barely coming into
view, these paintings picture reluctantly.

   Surrounded by raw linen, the figure in *Summer Nap*, 2017
(see p. 34), curls into itself, oscillating between viscous colour and
personhood. One stroke, fat and wet, is caressed onto sticky others,
but the whole refuses to be smoothed into a firmer illusion. The
paint pile lies fugitive, resting, and vulnerable against a dry dune of
dun linen.

   Draney describes her signature unpainted expanses as door-
ways for viewers to enter so that they can contemplate the scene
while bringing their own stories to the work. In addition, because
she works from memory—not painting the events live and rarely
from photographs—the untouched spaces suggest a refusal to picture anything she is uncertain of. She would rather leave an absence
than commit an error to memory: "I don't want to put anything in
there that isn't sort of really true to that memory, so that I'm only
articulating that part that is true for me, resonant for me, and then I
leave the rest blank."[2] It is a wonder that there is paint anywhere
at all, so great is her concern for fidelity and her uncertainty over
whether it can be achieved.

   I enter the work, contemplative and with my own stories.
Here, feeling as unmoored as the napper. There, transported to the
cabin of my youth. Now, remembering my first car accident. In
my mind, but also aware of being reminded by another. Hovering
between figure and disfigure, revelation and concealment, Draney
searches with her brush for a tentative presence. The mission?
"Just trying to get closer to true."[3] While truth aspires to settlement,
getting "closer to true" requires adjusting to the right position. Her
brush follows trails rather than marking points of arrival.

   Draney's subjects are elusive—close to her but less available
for others. Because she wants us to seek rather than capture her
subjects, she presents people but rarely their whereabouts. Her

1 National Gallery of Canada, "The 2016 Sobey Art Award - Brenda Draney," YouTube video, February 1, 2017, 2:18, https://www.youtube.com/watch?v=IN07t79nHUQ.

2 National Gallery of Canada, "The 2016 Sobey Art Award - Brenda Draney."

3 This quote and the preceding paraphrases are from National Gallery of Canada, "The 2016 Sobey Art Award - Brenda Draney."

provisional response to the paradox of the desire to share yet protect is the glimpse. To those familiar with her realm, a flash, fragment, or gesture is enough to evoke a whole. She says that her ideal viewers are people she grew up with in Slave Lake, Alberta, agreeing that those with similar small-town backgrounds are also likely to recognize the imagery and have it resonate.

While not quite her ideal viewer, I, like Draney, grew up in Edmonton—though nearly a generation earlier. The faux-wood panelling and the brass and wood ceiling fan in *Cut*, 2022 (see p. 13), transport me to that city in the 1970s. I can smell the unseen shag carpet embedded with the scent of dog and cooking and Nilodor. The painting reminds me of how hot the Prairies get in the summer. In a region with only a few months of scorching heat, air conditioning was an extravagance. Only the wealthy would dare the expense and acrimony. For many, the Zellers appliance is now considered kitschy, in the sense of aspiring to a higher class but falling short. In combination with the panelling, the painting both records a reality and dares a classist judgment. While the scene may be retrospective, Draney's gaze is never nostalgic. In fact, we might be looking at a present room undisturbed by revision. For me, there and then, wood panelling suggested the back-to-the-land movement—a desire to be surrounded by wood(s) while living in the city, even if only a veneer.

Another resonance: Draney is First Nations, and I am Métis. My great-great-grandparents, Laurent and Eleanor, settled Edmonton in 1874 after fleeing Red River following the collapse of the first Red River Resistance. Their land, still called Garneau, was, along with all of the other Métis river lots, soon swallowed by the city. Growing up, I often imagined their lives, their shift from a Red River cart to motor car. Perhaps wood panelling means something a little different to urban Indigenous Peoples—less a fad than a melancholic effort to reconnect.

While she is sure to announce her Indigeneity in her interviews, and every article refers to her connection to Sawridge First Nation, Draney does not explicitly foreground Indigenous issues in her interviews, statements, or paintings. Like every social identity, there is an aspect of being First Nations that is about display, about being legible to others. But that does not appear to interest her here. She is a witness. An interested, empathetic observer who aspires to record faithfully rather than to promote, explain, or contextualize. She is not looking to showcase conventional traces of Indigeneity. She shows what she knows: familiar people living their lives. While viewers may thread the fragments into a story, the artist avoids an explicit twining of these strands to larger historical and political narratives.

The range of skin tones and facial structures in Draney's works seem observed rather than illustrated. These folks are. They are not representing. While the flesh colour in many is a few shades darker than the usual Euro-North American artist's palette, not everyone pictured is certainly Indigenous or white. Hers is a mixed realm. While there is no regalia or other signifiers of traditional First Nations culture, something subtle but just right animates her figures.

The figure in *Dart*, 2017 (see p. 46), relaxed but alert, indirect eye contact, cigarette; he not only looks Native but like a specific type. The hunched figure in *Visit*, 2021 (see p. 42), watching TV while feigning disinterest at the cops at the door. The loud 70s couch, another cigarette, more wood panelling. I recognize these people, places, and attitudes.

Draney is perhaps best known for her tent paintings, offering glimpses of seeming vacationers but actually recalling folks from her home community of Slave Lake who were displaced by flood (1988) and fire (2011), and the unhoused in Edmonton living in a tent city. I feel these paintings. While never unhoused, in the late 1960s and early 70s, my family attended a community church in the Marian Centre beside Edmonton's recent tent city. Throughout my youth, I played chess and cards with the men there and in the nearby park. It was a need for safety, privacy, and dignity that kept many I talked to from shelters. A number of Draney's tent paintings— *Tent City*, 2010 (see p. 59), and *Orange Tent*, 2020 (see p. 25), for example— are abstract fragments that evoke events without invading privacy. Those depicted may recognize themselves in the paintings, and remember those days, but they are unlikely to be recognized by gallery-goers. They are glimpsed rather than the subjects of surveillance. Their lives are not simplified by narration: "Part of my hesitation in answering questions about my paintings is because I think a lot about how much I should disclose about the specifics of narrative. It feels a little heavy-handed or dramatic to say this but I'm trying to cultivate desire. If I confirm it for you, you can put it to bed. And if I tell you you're wrong, then I've pushed you out and said you don't understand it, you're not invited in."[4]

As with her other scenes of daily life, Draney avoids exploitation. And yet she is driven to make visible, to show just enough so viewers can piece things together. Knowing, however, that the scene they produce is not *the* event but their rendering. The desire Draney cultivates is a longing for meaning held in a space of suspense between the actual experience of another and the viewer's empathetic fiction.

Flood, 2009 (see p. 22), shows a green pickup truck fleeing the canvas. The white ground's emptiness or erasure figures a flood. It reminds me of Spanish painter Francisco Goya's dog (*The Dog*, c. 1819–23), whose small head peeks out from a vast undefined plane that is at once the real ground and its illusion. And what is going on in *Strange Invitation*, 2020 (see p. 33)? It might be a tent painting. Is the reclining figure wearing shades in a sleeping bag? Is the strange invitation an offer to join him in the sack or on the lawn chair that faces away from him? Draney explains that her paintings are based on shared and personal memories. Which memory is *Strange Invitation* based on? It might mean a great deal to her, but the viewer will never know. She explains that when she is alone in her studio, painting, she contemplates her relations and connections. The feelings are there, in her, but are they recorded in the brush strokes? I know artists, deep feelers, whose greatest thrill is to have artworks displayed in public that contain personal content that remains unread because, in the absence of a story,

4   Robert Enright, "Put the Sky Until the Sky Stops: An Interview with Brenda Draney," *Border Crossings* 36, no. 3 (Fall 2017): 69–73.

5   *Canadian Art*, "A Conversation with Brenda Draney," Facebook, July 20, 2018, https://www.facebook. com/canadianart/videos/a-conversation-with-brenda-draney/1015627-7494405630/.

their signifiers can only be connected to meanings in the maker's mind. It is like Catholic confession: the secret is revealed but nothing leaves the chamber.

In an interview with *Canadian Art*, Draney describes the unpainted areas in her paintings as the "liminal space between a secret and a mystery … a secret, the thing you don't disclose, you don't say … mystery is a thing you can't quite articulate. Maybe you don't know that you're withholding, or maybe you don't know how to put language around it. I think that's what I try to do, is go to the spaces where we can't quite put language around."[5] The language associated with her works, their titles, are as spare as the images: *Toast*, *Rest*, *Summer Nap*, *Pray*, *Rose*, *Flood*, *Theatre*, *Julie*, etc. Most are single, literal names rather than descriptions, metaphors, or poetry. As with her minimalist paint gestures, she indicates something without alluding to its fuller meanings. Or, perhaps she is suggesting that such meanings are the product of language, of storytelling, rather than a true account. She seems to be hinting that the "secret," the "mystery," the "it" that cannot be wrapped in language might be swathed in paint. Perhaps she can clothe its shape without constricting "it" too much. Her skins are loose and fragmentary to afford breathing room and escape.

Analytic perspective is the crown jewel of Western art and Enlightenment thinking. Draney's refusal to let its grid organize her untouched territories is a rejection of ocularcentrism, the colonial gaze that must draw and quarter space before conquering it.

When first seeing Draney's work, my colonized mind longed to associate it with white male artists: Draney's *Toast*, 2022 (see p. 38), is a little of David Hockney, some Henri Matisse here and there, and Luc Tuymans everywhere. Having gone to art school, she is certain to have known and absorbed the lessons of many. However, we can find more fruitful form *and* content influences among her Indigenous Elders and siblings: some of Alex Janvier's lyrical lines on raw linen, for example, and a lot of Annie Pootoogook's forthright rendering of a child's experience in *Rose*, 2019 (see p. 30), a scene inscribed with multiple meanings that circles around in the mind, deep into adulthood.

While there are, of course, infinite personal secrets and mysteries, the collective secret and mystery that haunts this land, Northern Turtle Island (also known as Canada), is the legacy of colonialism. Every Indigenous person is affected and every settler is distorted. So, Draney's paintings, though they have a specificity, also express a shared haunting. Her incomplete figures and settings, their difficulty in coming to form, fear of resolution, also figures a common state. In "Altars of Sacrifice: Re-membering Basquiat," American author and activist bell hooks (1952–2021) contemplates the paintings of Jean-Michel Basquiat (1960–1988): "The black body as Basquiat shows it is incomplete, not fulfilled, never a full image" because it is "commodified, appropriated, made to 'serve' the interests of white masters. … Content to be only what the oppressors want, this black image can never be fully self-actualized. It must always be represented as fragmented. Expressing a firsthand knowledge of the way assimilation and objectification lead to isolation, Basquiat's black male figures stand alone and apart. They are not whole people."[6]

Even if she isn't familiar with Basquiat's work, Draney's methodology appears to derive from a similar experience as Saulteaux Anishinaabe artist Robert Houle's *Sandy Bay Residential School Series*, 2009. These works are similarly rough, expressionist fragments floating in emptied space: part of a building, a cot. They, too, are reluctant to figure too much, cautious about revealing secrets in words and converting them into stories—as happened on an industrial scale during the Truth and Reconciliation commission.[7] There is a peculiar suite of six oil-stick paintings on paper that especially resonate. They show a shack from various angles. It is as if the viewer and artist are circling the building but never approaching it. The feeling is not of the reconnaissance of an unknown thing but of revisiting something familiar, orbiting around something with energy, a space that cannot be approached without consequence. During a pained talk at the exhibition's opening, Houle hinted at what happened there. His words were like his sketches—offering just enough to co-produce mental images that burden still, but not enough to claim we understand.

Paint is a skin to clothe memory. It reveals but also protects. If the counterfeit is too convincing, too realistic, it sacrifices complexity for legibility and the illustration can be mistaken for what it represents (and conceals). Most representational painting claims to represent some absent thing. But every painting, however *trompe l'oeil*, also hides a forest of absences. Taking this phenomenon seriously, "trying to get closer to true," Brenda Draney offers shades that refuse to fool anyone.

6   bell hooks, "Altars of Sacrifice: Remembering Basquiat," in *Outlaw Culture: Resisting Representations* (New York: Routledge, 1994), 31.

7   The Truth and Reconciliation Commission, a government-sanctioned body, was commissioned in 2008. Its purpose was to hear testimony from residential school survivors within the Indigenous, Métis, and Inuit communities; compile a report on the atrocities committed and the intergenerational effects of the system; and recommend policy changes and foster educational programs that would prevent such atrocities from ever happening again. "What are the Truth and Reconciliation Commission's 94 Calls to Action & How Are We Working Toward Achieving Them Today?" Reconciliation Education, https://www.reconciliationeducation.ca/what-are-truth-and-reconciliation-commision-94-calls-to-action.

WHY WOULDN'T OURS?
Souvankham Thammavongsa

A memory is something we have to ourselves. Even the people who were there at the time don't remember the exact same details. Even now, where I am and what I am doing, I cannot say with absolute certainty it will become a memory. I won't know until years from now. And if I forget, who will it matter to but to me? Memory is so deeply personal to the person who holds it. Not necessarily to those who are in its material. These days, all I have are memories. I want to tell people about them—these memories—every chance I get. I want to tell even if it's out of context. I want every sentence I make to begin with "My brother." It's what grief does to you. It places you out of context, and then also, you never want to go back to being in context if it means not getting to remember the things you want to remember.

My brother died a few months ago. A lot of people die, and we don't know about them. When it's personal and when it's this close, we have nothing but the desire to remember the memories we have of them. My brother's death has made memories of him so vivid. When I think of these things, it is as if I am there at the moment the memory was made. It doesn't take much to make me remember. A smell. A sound. A child in a stroller. A pregnant woman. Someone with black hair. I don't know Brenda Draney. I didn't know of her paintings until I was told about them. What struck me most about them was Draney's use of negative space. I don't like the word "negative" to describe space. Especially when I look at that space and find myself filling it with my own memories. What my mind fills it with is not negative at all. When I look at Draney's paintings, I feel I can look as long as I want. I don't feel like I am exhausting anyone with my memories. The blank space on the canvas is where I put my memories. No one sees them, of course. They see colour and figures and objects and patterns. The things Draney paints come from her memory. I know she can't see my memories because they are mine, yet the space to have them and put them there with hers feels something like grace.

There's a painting with the back of a blue car (see *Accord*, 2021, p. 67). I am told it's a painting of a Honda Accord. My parents had this blue car, but it was a Toyota Corolla. It was the first thing they bought once they saved up enough money from their first job in Canada. I always sat in the back seat of that car with my brother. Him on the left side, right behind the driver. It was the car our parents picked us up in when they finished a shift at work. And the car they drove back to the factory in when they had to work overtime. There was no one to look after us. So my father pushed back the front passenger seat and put me and my brother on the floor and covered us with a blanket. My brother could fall asleep anywhere, and did. I was scared, but I wasn't alone. I didn't cry because I had a brother, and for him I had to be brave and keep watch. I couldn't tell time. A half hour or three hours seemed the same to me. They were both long, and after that time passed, it was always so dark outside. My parents would come out of the factory and give us the thing they had made inside it. Gumballs. My mom said it was like food but you could chew it forever. We were so proud of our parents. They made this good thing in the world.

In another of Draney's paintings, there's a figure of a small girl in a blue bathing suit (see *Julie*, 2010, p. 17). There's a bit of blood on the ground. I, too, had a blue bathing suit. I was nine when it happened to me. I had been running around in a creek. My mother said there might be leeches in the shallow water. "Be careful," she said. A few days later, I saw blood. I didn't know what it was exactly and thought it might have to do with the leeches. I was sure one had gone in there and was feasting on my insides. I went to my mother and told her about the blood. I said, "I think a leech went in there. Can you take it out?" She laughed and said, "Go put a pad on." I did. They were the cheap, bulky kind she liked to buy. When they got wet, the glue would come undone. One fell out during gym class when I was twelve. My brother heard about this and went to the corner store and bought me the expensive ones. He told me his friend's sisters wore them. "They protect against leaks," he said.

In another work, Draney has painted a wood panel behind a couch (see *Visit*, 2021, p. 42). I have seen that before. There's a picture of my brother and me the first day he was brought home from the hospital. My father is holding him. I am sitting, wondering what he is doing there and why he is wearing some of my clothes. No one explained to me who he was. I just knew now I wasn't the only one. The flowers on the couch remind me of the flowers on the carpet we had in our home. Having carpet in a home meant you were doing well. This carpet was where my brother and I sat every morning to catch the cartoons. After school, and on the weekends, we'd watch whatever was playing on television. There weren't a lot of channels then. Just thirteen. He'd stand by the television and press the buttons, and I got to choose. He would watch whatever I chose. Now when I see these movies and rewatch them, I remember my brother, the things that happened while we watched a movie, and not so much the movie itself. I remember we always sat cross-legged, side by side. When something exciting or scary happened, we'd turn to look at each other. I still turn and look now, at the exact same moments in the movie, but there is no one there. There is only the memory. And who to tell this memory to? It matters to no one but the one who holds it. And who will remember this when I do not?

When I get to Draney's painting of someone on a couch, alone, taking a nap (see *Rest*, 2021, p. 29), I think of my brother. How I wanted him to take a rest just like that. He was always so busy. Running around, making sure others were all right. Working. Even as a grown man with a job as a welder he would often return to my father's sign-making shop and work there because my father had asked him to. He had worked there since he was thirteen years old. At that age, he didn't skip school to go to the movies or hang out with friends. He skipped school to work with my father. They worked long hours. More than twelve hours. He was a boy working a man's job and hours. Even at forty-two he was doing my father's work.

There's a picture of us when my brother is two and I am four. He has the expression of an adult who is worried about the rent payments. My parents worried about the rent, and so did we. I had only

just come to learn that most people don't worry about rent until
they are at least twenty-six years old. If ever, really, if their parents
pay it. I look at this picture of my brother and think he's been worried
about something for too long, and it's too much. When my brother
died, I didn't go see his body. I was afraid. I didn't want to know that
my brother was dead. When I saw Draney's painting of bruised
legs (see *Legs*, 2022, p. 21)—just legs—I thought of my brother's
legs. They look like my brother's legs. I always wondered why there
were so many bruises and why he still had them all these years.
I know being dead means not being here. That I can't ever see my
brother again. And because of the way he died, I don't want to
believe he is somewhere suffering. He had enough of that. I don't believe in much but my own mind and the memories it holds. I trust that.

When I saw Draney's painting of a boy at the bottom of a small
staircase (see *Descendant*, 2013, p. 14), I thought about how he
looked a lot like my brother. When my family first came to Canada,
we lived in a basement. My first memory is of sitting on a stair. At
the top of that staircase was someone else's home. The person who
lived there always had a warm meal and a few pieces of chocolate
for me. It didn't take much for me to love someone. And that, really,
was all it took. I was two years old, and I would often knock on the
door at the top of the staircase. I once announced I was going to
live there. I thought I could choose for myself like that. But I was
told I did not belong to them. I belonged to my parents. The people
who lived at the bottom of the staircase. I didn't know how to speak
English then. But sometimes, even when the language doesn't make
sense to you, you can understand its tone. I was made to understand my responsibility to the people I belonged to. I didn't want to
belong to anyone. When I was seven, I told my mother, "I do not like
you." She laughed and said she didn't care because "I'm your mother."
She was someone to me, and I didn't have to like it.

My brother was not like me. He wanted to be good. He wanted
to be normal. He would do anything to belong, to be taken in. And
even when he did good or had the things that make you normal, he
never felt normal. He was always alone or felt alone, like the figures
in Draney's paintings. If you met my brother, even if he needed it,
he'd give you the best chair—that green chair (see *Strange Invitation*,
2020, p. 33). It's the kind of chair you take camping or you put under
your arm and fold out when you decide to go fishing. My brother
loved the outdoors because we saw so little of it growing up.

Once, we both made a wish on an airplane. It was the only
moving light in the sky, and we thought it was a shooting star. There
were so many planes, and they were all so slow. They stayed long
enough for us to make our wish. And we asked for so many things.
When we finally learned they were not shooting stars and that we've
never actually seen a shooting star and that all our wishes were
wasted, my brother insisted that a wish is a wish, and it's never a
waste. He said it was better to make a wish on a thing made of
metal and plastic flying through the sky. That thing was someone
else's wish and it came true. Why wouldn't ours?

IN SEARCH OF MYSTERY
    Graham Foy

    *We're fascinated by the words—but where we meet is in the
    silence behind them.*[1]
    —Ram Dass

Like a wide-open sky—the expanse of nothingness that frames
a landscape—it is the emptiness of existence that allows room for
what is to emerge from Brenda Draney's personal narratives.
Having grown up in Alberta, I am deeply familiar with the idea of
large, empty spaces. My memories of the western Canadian
province are framed by open landscapes and an almost infinite
horizon line stretching outward from suburban Calgary. As a
filmmaker, I am drawn to these expanses, both visually and
psychologically. In my first feature film, *The Maiden* (2022), I, like
Draney, drew heavily from personal memory. My process as
a screenwriter and filmmaker is rooted in a sense of rediscovery,
looking back through wide vistas of time to create something
new based on the past. This process tends to reveal empty gaps in
psychological space—things are forgotten, left out, reinterpreted.
These gaps leave room for mystery and imagination; they inform
something that, in my own work, feels closer to personal mythology
than factual history. It's this sense of mystery and the unknown
that I believe offers space for something emotionally true, an access
point to a specific personal narrative that might reach something
more transcendent or universal. It is these spaces between ambiguity
and specificity in Draney's work, like the breaks between the words
on a page, that invite the viewer to respond, participate, and
converse with the artist and enter her intimate scenes.

In Draney's 2023 exhibition *Drink from the river*, we are
encouraged to witness and contemplate both a visual and a temporal
emptiness. The physical emptiness on canvas is also evocative of
an internal one, a space in time created by the artist's looking back
at memory and conjuring up an in-between. A place that is inspired
by real observation, which in the painting exists in fragments, spun
together with a vivid combination of emotion, colour, and form. In
these depictions of memory there is both beauty and haunting pain
in the decay or reflection of the past, like a mould that reveals its
rich colours as time goes by.

In Draney's paintings, we are challenged as viewers to
examine the comfort of familiar domestic spaces and scenes in
addition to the traumatic, searching for clues in the specificity
of details, like the repeated rendering of the Colonial Revival–styled
upholstery of a couch that helps bind a narrative web. In *Visit*,
2021 (see p. 42), we encounter the figures of two police officers floating in space beside the aforementioned couch and a figure at
the edge of the cushions with their back hunched. The placement of
the figures arouses the possibility of narratives of encroachment,
the invasion of a personal space, with clearly drawn lines indicating
boundaries. The police figures float outside of this well-defined
space, anchored as uninvited visitors. The use of negative space in

1 Ram Dass (@BabaRamDass), "We're fascinated by the words—but where we meet is in the silence behind them," Twitter, May 26, 2016, 9:16 PM, https://twitter.com/BabaRamDass/status/736003011760136194?lang=en.

this image helps ground the figures and their sense of place and imparts specificity to the scene; but what is left out also adds to the scene's complexity, refuting the ability to be read with a singular, causal narrative, especially when seen in the context of the exhibition as a whole.

In *Rose*, 2019 (see p. 30), we see a child looking in on a man and a woman in bed, a trail of rose petals behind them. Again, negative space separates the personal space of the bed from the position of the child. The child sees the couple and the couple see the child, but there is no clear invitation, evoking questions of belonging. However, there's still a deep sense of mystery, one that draws us closer and provokes self-reflection rather than revealing concrete answers.

The in-between spaces in Draney's work manifest the question of where one belongs. In *Evacuation*, 2013 (see p. 10), an unclothed figure stands in front of a house and in front of bright, violent flashes of yellow. In *Flood*, 2009 (see p. 22), a dark mark surrounded by a white void may evoke the emptiness that remains after a disastrous event. In *Tent City*, 2010 (see p. 59), we discover an image of tents obscured by an off-white void. Is this someone's home? The location of a displacement? Or something more symbolic? The repeated tent imagery within Draney's works foregrounds notions of exterior and interior space, psychological and physical belonging. There is a rhythm throughout the paintings that cycles between trauma, the possibility of displacement, and the idea of intimacy, home, and where one can be at peace. These scenes floating in or partially obscured by a void often conjure up psychological space in addition to physical representation.

As in a film, each image presented in Draney's exhibition offers a fragment of a larger picture, one that reveals something more whole than each individual piece alone. In memory, unlike most films, these fragments often appear in a non-linear sequence. When seen together, time becomes fluid. It can be impossible to decipher personal narrative in absolutes, but in the case of *Drink from the river*, the importance of singular narrative arrangements and certainty is eclipsed by a thematic pulse and haunting tone. There's a ghostly quality to the exhibition. Half-filled-in spaces create a stage for figures and objects to emerge through the fog of time. Are they visitors from another life? The shadows of past events? These images leave room for personal connection; they dance with life in a way that leaves room for the viewer's own experiences to intermingle.

Draney's scenes often contain a quotidian magic. *Orange Tent*, 2020 (see p. 25), is rendered in a simplicity reminiscent of the landscapes painted by American artist Richard Diebenkorn (1922–1993). The couch returns in *Sleep*, 2008 (see p. 56), and *Rest*, 2021 (see p. 29), which depict figures lying down in domestic spaces. Moments of everyday stillness are given the same importance as bigger events depicted in *Evacuation* and *Flood*. Time itself flows like water in *Drink from the river*, with undulating currents of intimacy and trauma blending together into one fluid, rearrangeable stream. Linearity is left behind in favour of a more democratic view of causality. Instead of one event influencing the next, we are compelled to see the connections between the layered whole. Like a time traveller whose smallest misstep will alter the entirety of their future, each moment depicted in the exhibition shares an egalitarian connection. There is no before or after, no past and no future, only the mystery of *now*, depicted in each image and connecting us to an empathetic gaze into another world.

Draney's work makes us question how we got here, how we know what we know, and firmly grounds us in our collective present. The river of images takes us down unexpected streams, twisting and turning, revealing no singular story; instead, it suggests an interconnected web of lives and moments we ourselves could pass by or experience. A collage of moments that, like life, never amounts to a tidy grand finale. Nonetheless, the figures in Draney's paintings are anchored by a form of narrative empathy that affirms the consciousness of life, many of which are depicted in moments of introspection. In *Vanity*, 2019 (see p. 41), a naked figure faces away from their reflection, gazing off into an empty abyss. In *Summer Nap*, 2017 (see p. 34), another solitary figure lays at rest, sleeping in a warm void. In *Dart*, 2017 (see p. 46), and *Teenager*, 2019 (see p. 37), figures take time to themselves with a cigarette. In *The Righteous*, 2010 (see p. 60), and *Pray*, 2020 (see p. 26), figures face the viewer, yet both carry a sense that the gaze is internal. In *Shan*, 2013 (see p. 55), the character's eyes are closed, oriented away from the viewer, and the figure's head appears to be leaning against a wall. Again, the gaze feels inward. These are internal narratives. We recognize these moments from our own lives, but each contains an inner world impossible to fully decipher, meant to be felt more than concretely understood.

These moments of pause are complex in their ambiguity. Many of the figures in *Drink from the river* are either turned away from view or rendered with an expression that directs us to inner experience, the character's and our own. There's no dialogue to guide us, no indication of what came before or after; these are everyday moments that exude empathy. In these character-driven scenes, the poetry of the world is left alone. There are no grand gestures, no blockbuster life events, but instead a genuine understanding and confirmation of the presence of life.

This is the magic of Brenda Draney's work. To dance with the flow of memories and life, to gently assemble its randomness of scattered places, events, and forms into a poetic narrative that has no firm beginning and no tidy ending. These are spaces and moments that overlap and suggest the possibility of experiencing intimacy and trauma on equal terms, weaving time, existence, and chance into an earthly truth that invites us to dive deeper into our own consciousness.

EMPTINESS IS THE NATURE OF ALL THINGS
    Ken Lum

I first met artist Brenda Draney at the Banff Centre for Arts and
Creativity in 2010. My initial impression of her paintings was that
they were not fully realized, with their sketchily defined vignettes
floating like islands in a sea of undifferentiated canvas. There was,
however, a quality about them that expressed her ambition to
tap into what French psychoanalyst Jacques Lacan (1901–1981)
described as "the malaise of the society in which we live."[1] Like
Lacan's definition of psychoanalysis, Draney's artistic practice is
concerned with "whatever is not going right," and it is "prone to
all sorts of ambiguities."[2] I realize now that the seemingly incomplete
character of her paintings for the sake of an uncertain status is
precisely the point.

Draney paints with a broad brushstroke, generating a formal
flatness of image, but this lack of detail transmits the idea of a depth
that cannot be known. Her paintings are fraught with an ambiguity
regarding the said and the unsaid. They reveal as much as they
hide, like a shadow play that comes in and out of visibility. Her
scenarios often portray individuals alone or in small groups, while
the titles of the works provide little contextualization: *Tent*, 2012,
and *Vacuum*, 2019, refer only to the objects pictured, and figures
are identified, if at all, by their first names only (*Betty*, 2012,
and *Carrie*, 2019). ① ② ③ ④ ↗

Draney's vignettes overflow with possible narratives that
hemorrhage into the empty spaces of her canvases, calling attention
to the dissipative nature of existential nothingness. Depicted is a
disconsolate world, cheerless and banal, as though to underline the
Buddhist sutra that emptiness is the nature of all things. In Buddhism,
emptiness is a practice of body and mind to achieve full consciousness, but in Draney's paintings, emptiness speaks of the expunging
of individual will from consciousness in a soul-destroying world.
The open casket funeral in *Wake*, 2019, positions the deceased as
the most wholly rendered figure in the composition. To his left
hovers a barely demarcated trio of mourners. Next to the casket is
a figure with a hockey stick, localizing the scene as Canadian.
The rest of the painting's surface is blank. *Wake* operates in an
opposite way to French painter Gustave Courbet's *A Burial at Ornans*,
1849–50, where a surfeit of details culminates around a burial
hole in which no body is visible.

Reviewers of Draney's work have often placed emphasis
on how her vignettes are derived from memories. Indeed, she has
talked about how "there is usually a memory as a starting point."[3]
However, this is an insufficient response to the visual effect of the
vignettes, which appear unfixed, even to the canvases themselves.
This floating quality articulates a sense of existence on the periph-
ery of the elaborate system of power and privilege called society.
In *Rest*, 2021 (see p. 29), a barely delineated figure lies on a worn-out
sofa. Next to the sofa is an old chair. The figure merges, in colour
and line, with the contours of the sofa. The image is far from
languorous with its shock of jagged lines, fecal-brown colour, and

1   Jordan Skinner, "'There can be no crisis of psychoanalysis' Jacques Lacan interviewed in 1974," Verso Books (blog), July 22, 2014, https://www.versobooks.com/blogs/1668-there-can-be-no-crisis-of- psychoanalysis-jacques-lacan-interviewed-in-1974.

2   Skinner, "'There can be no crisis of psychoanalysis.'"

3   Email exchange between the author and Draney, October 23, 2022.

4   Giorgio Agamben, *What Is an Apparatus? and Other Essays*, trans. David Kishik and Stefan Pedatella (Stanford: Stanford University Press, 2009), 41.

5   The full text of Benjamin's unfinished writings was published in English translation in 1999. See Walter Benjamin, *The Arcades Project*, trans. Howard Eiland and Kevin McLaughlin (Cambridge, MA: Belknap Press of Harvard University Press, 1999).

figure emptied of form. Unlike Spanish artist Francisco Goya's *The Sleep of Reason Produces Monsters*, ca. 1799, Draney's figure reveals no dreams, just repose for the basic function of getting to the next day. As such, *Rest* reveals a deep truth about the moneyed economy and the wreckage it bears on the most vulnerable bodies.

The figure in *Rest* embodies a persistent allegory running through all of Draney's work. It is the allegory of a racialized coloniality that has continued over generations of time and continues to press down on those deemed subalterns. In this sense, her work calls up Italian philosopher Giorgio Agamben's idea of "contemporariness," a form of deeper consciousness of existence within the same time that can often produce insights about the world that are profoundly discomforting. As Agamben explains,

> Contemporariness is, then, a singular relationship to one's time, which adheres to it and, at the same time, keeps a distance from it. More precisely, it is that relationship with time that adheres to it through a disjunction and an anachronism. Those who coincide too well with the epoch, those who are perfectly tied to it in every respect, are not contemporaries, precisely because they do not manage to see it; they are not able to firmly hold their gaze on it.[4]

It is their "contemporariness" that gives Draney's works a sense of speaking truth to power regarding the problem of individual and collective marginalization. Her paintings evoke an oneiric quality, but not in the enchanting sense of an indelible dream. Rather, they are like uncertain memories that oscillate between the will to remember and the will to forget. Their indeterminate quality is enhanced by recurring unpainted areas, which are symbolically important because they represent a space free from codes of the prevailing social order. They also express the notion that a more harmonious world is not possible to articulate. In art, there are many examples of emptiness expressing a space of symbolic potentiality. For example, in French painter Jacques-Louis David's *The Death of Marat*, 1793, the entire top half of the painting is a green monochrome, the greenness charged with Marat's post-monarchic ideals. In *The Righteous*, 2010 (see p. 60), Draney depicts only the face, arms, and legs of a seated male figure, while the rest of the canvas is left unpainted. The extensive areas of blank surface function like monochromatic space, much like the top half of David's *Marat*, in which resides a multiplicity of possible meanings.

Draney's floating and fragmentary vignettes call up German philosopher Walter Benjamin (1892–1940) and his concept of "remembrance," rooted in the phenomenon of blushing, a fragment of emotion that can issue suddenly from a sense of shame or anger, but that can also relapse suddenly back into the realm of a vast social sphere of alienated existence. Like the *Arcades Project*, Benjamin's incomplete collection of writings written between 1927 and 1940,[5] Draney's patchwork of imagery is like assembling fragments imbued with transience, or like amorphous fragments that articulate the cruelty of a world disconnected from the desires of people. Yet, it is this cruelty that becomes the creative process for Draney. It is a cruelty that is at once shameful and engendering of shame, for, according to Benjamin, claims of the hubristic triumph of capitalism over nature are annihilated in the blushing of shame.

> Because the red of blushing does not stain the skin neither inner discord nor inner disintegration appear on the surface in it. This blushing conveys nothing at all of the interior. Were it to do so, this would be enough to induce a new shame again: that of discovering humanity in a frail soul. Instead—as is actually the case—in blushing all reasons for shame, everything internal, is extinguished. The redness of shame does not well up out of the interior (and that ascending redness of shame, of which one occasionally speaks, is not the thing that ashames), rather, the redness of shame is poured over the ashamed person from outside, from above; and just as it expunges his disgrace, so does it withdraw him from disgracefulness. For in the darkened reddening that shame pours over him he is withdrawn from the gazes of people, as if under a veil. Whoever is ashamed sees nothing, and he alone is also not seen.[6]

The "incompleteness" of Draney's paintings has the effect of a blush, like the slight pink stain on the side of the face portrayed in *The Righteous*. Her vignettes function like stains in the way that the depicted elements are loosely patched together. The term "stain" is a shortening of "distain," from the Old French *desteindre* for "tinge with a color different from the natural one."[7] The noun was first recorded in the mid-sixteenth century in the sense of "defilement" and "disgrace." French philosopher Georges Bataille (1897–1962) saw stains as sites of liberation precisely because of their power to defile and convolute all fixed historical and methodological disciplines and discursive boundaries.[8] Stains exude an overflowing violent potential because they are like the marks left by the discharge of feces, marks that are usually suppressed from acknowledgement yet must be confronted and embraced to be free from the symbolic order. According to Bataille, a stain is always approximate to violence and eroticism, the latter characterized by an eschatological sensuality that risks the overflowing of social taboos.[9] Draney's paintings, with their murky islands of delineation, flutter between overflow and containment. They hover between the dichotomies of presence and absence, legibility and hiddenness, form and shapelessness, and remembrance and forgetting. Like a Bataillean stain, Draney's vignettes signify the illicit trace of something real that is difficult to remove unless accepted for what it is. The stains of oppression, violence, and trauma permeate all of Draney's work. In *Repose*, 2013, the torso of a figure is demarcated by a smear of red paint that looks like a thick dollop of blood. A second rendering of the figure's head appears in spectral form above their body. (5) ↗

Draney paints a daily stream of life marked by her formation in Slave Lake, located in northern Alberta. Her images are like whirlpools of uncertainty, and this uncertainty belies the very palpable conditions of existence of those portrayed. In *Bear Trails*, 2022, a group of individuals sit in the woods. The painting makes explicit reference to French painter Édouard Manet's *Le Déjeuner*

1   Jordan Skinner, "There can be no crisis of psychoanalysis: Jacques Lacan interviewed in 1974," Verso Books (blog), July 22, 2014, https://www.verso[illegible].

[2–3 illegible]

4   Giorgio Agamben, *Nudities*, trans. David Kishik and Stefan Pedatella (Stanford, CA: Stanford University Press, 2010), 4[illegible].

[5] Walter Benjamin, [illegible] which was published in English as [illegible] and Vance [illegible] upon the [illegible], trans. [illegible] McLaughlin (Cambridge, MA: Harvard University Press, 1998).

6 Walter Benjamin, "On Shame" (ca. 1919–20), *Gesammelte Shriften*, vol. 6, trans. Jacob Bard-Rosenberg (Frankfurt am Main: Suhrkamp, 1972), 69–71.

7 "Stain," Encyclopedia.com, https://www. encyclopedia.com/medicine/divisions- diagnostics-and-procedures/medicine/stain.

8 For further reading on Bataille's notion of the stain, see Georges Bataille, *Visions of Excess: Selected Writings 1927–1939*, ed. Allan Stoekl, trans. Allan Stoekl, Carl R. Lovitt, and Donald M. Leslie Jr. (Minneapolis: University of Minnesota Press, 1985).

9 Bataille, *Visions of Excess*.

sur l'herbe, 1863, but the reference is a negation. Draney's female figure faces in the opposite direction from her counterpart in *Le Déjeuner sur l'herbe,* and there is anxiety in the mien of the well-defined face of the lone woman. The group sits in a *terrain vague* reminiscent of the interstices of a partially cleared forest. It is not a bucolic image. Moreover, Draney's title suggests not just danger but a fraught relationship between Indigenous Peoples and nature perpetrated by colonial genocide. ⑥ ↗

The banality Draney depicts is not merely that of everyday ordinariness. She depicts the banality of lives shackled by the rules of capital, by social immobility, and by racialized othering. It is the banality of lives shaped by perpetual and reinforcing administrative and cultural violence. When I speak about banality, I am not referring to the ennui of middle-class living. I am not speaking about Madame Bovary or Walter Mitty. I am speaking about the banality of poverty, the dullness of marginalization, and the claustrophobia of racism, especially of Canada's most oppressed peoples. Poverty, marginalization, and racism are so everyday that they are often barely noticed.

I sense that Draney is not interested in giving voice to the marginalized by reducing the narrative to simply that of generational trauma, which often reifies the narrative of dependency and helplessness. Rather, she is interested in grappling with the ways that people live in the face of generational hegemonic oppression. Her work does not gratify with the possibility of escape from an inhumane system. There is no redemptive pathway for her subjects to build wholeness from the world In which they are immersed. They are simply present in the world. To represent a subject in its entirety runs the risk of reducing it to a kind of cliché, the ultimate signifier of the banal. This is why the abstract, the blank, that which is unrepresented, is so important in Draney's work. The blank signifies the unfulfillment of a truly unequal and unjust society.

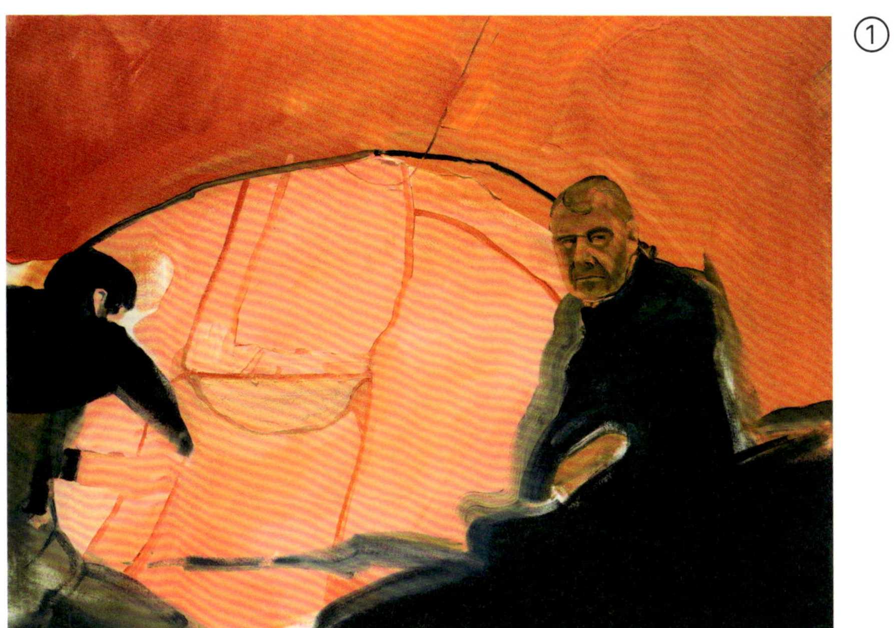

Tent
2012

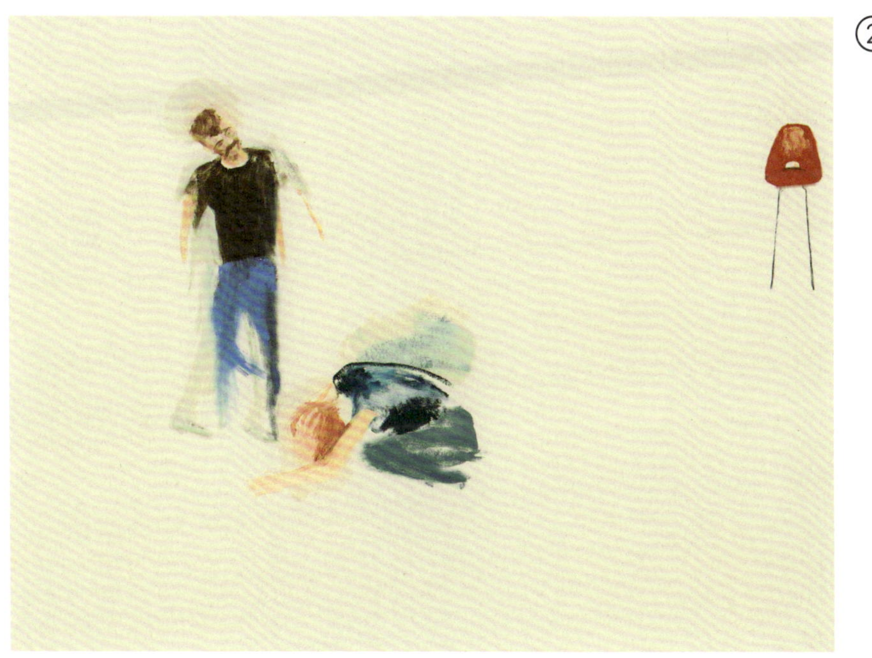

Vacuum
2019

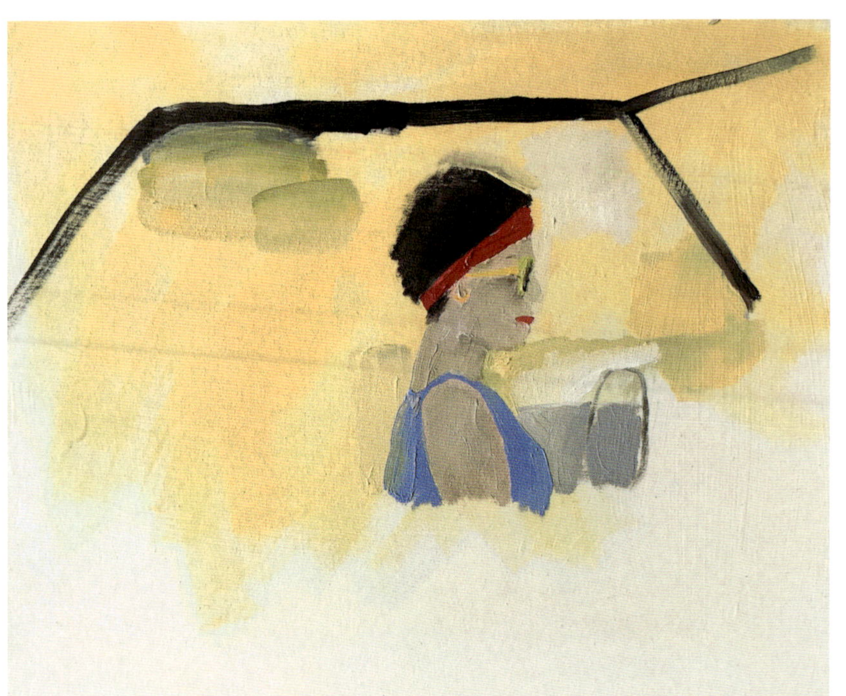

③

Betty
2012

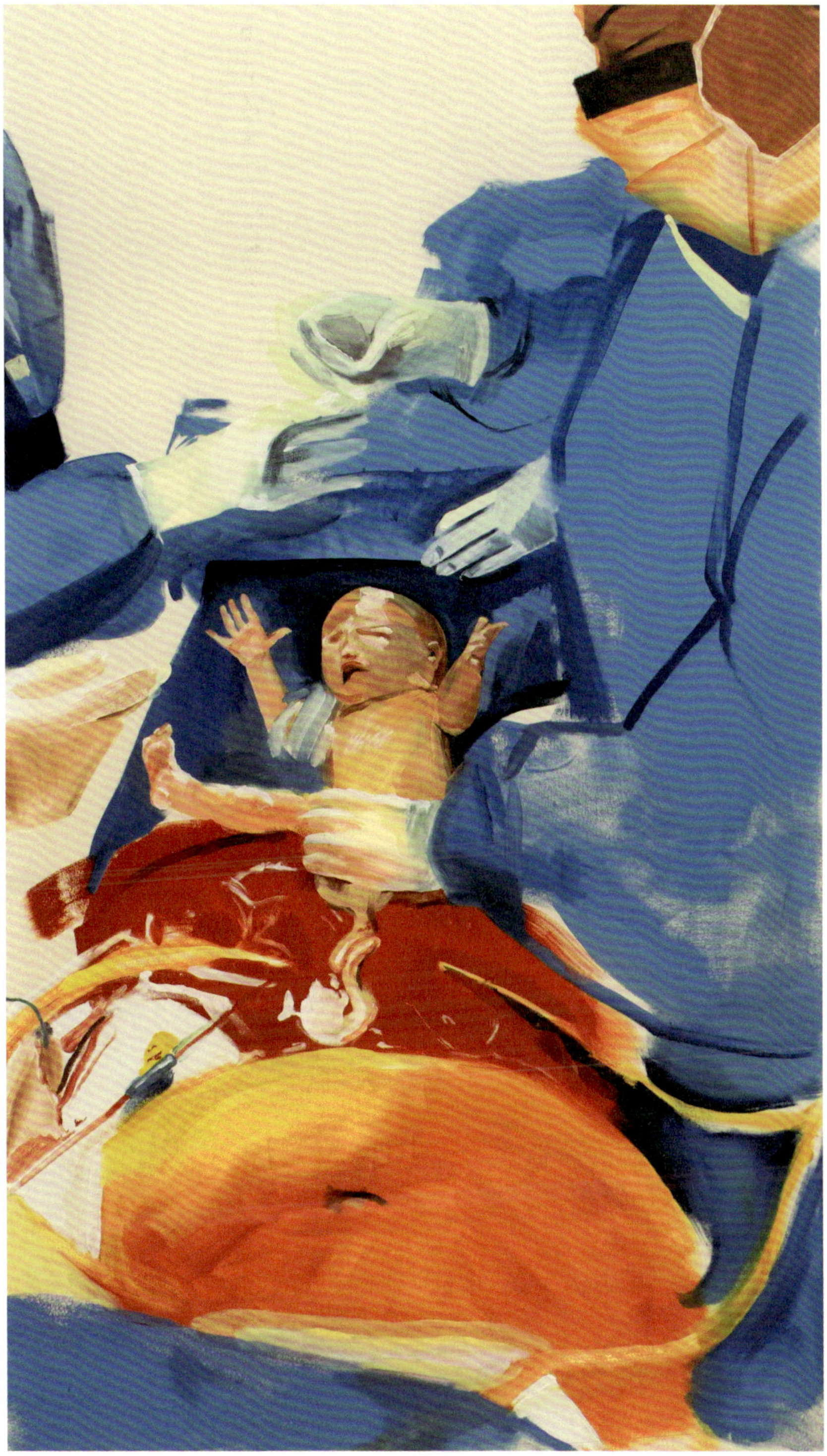

Carrie
2019

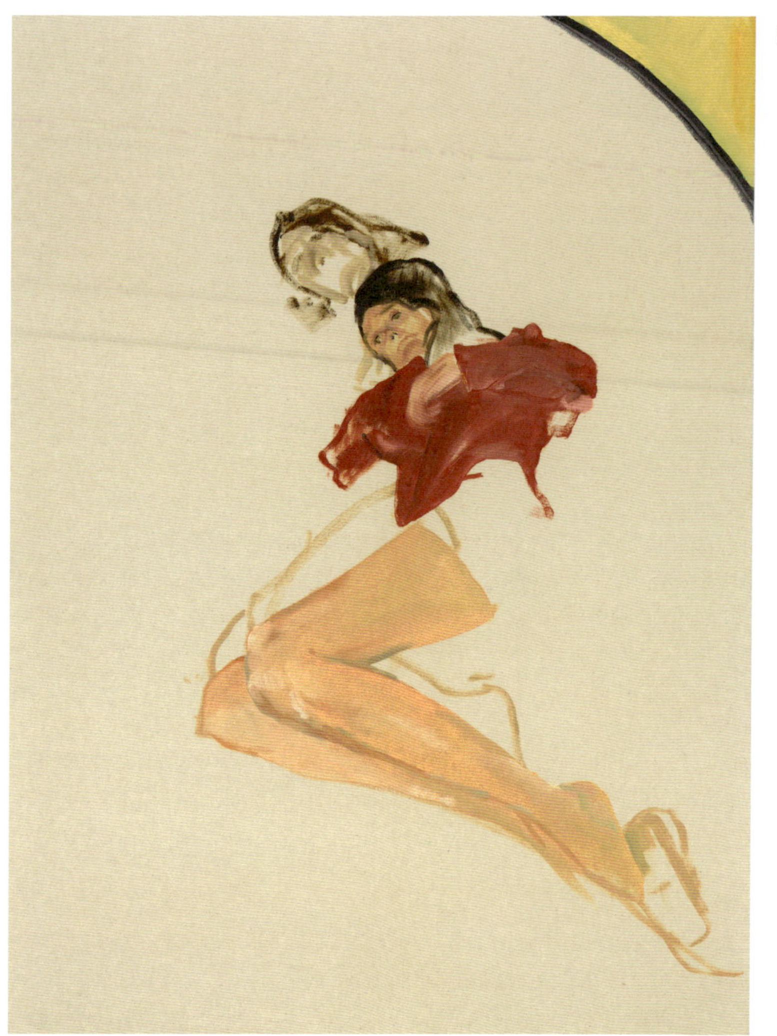

⑤

Repose
2013

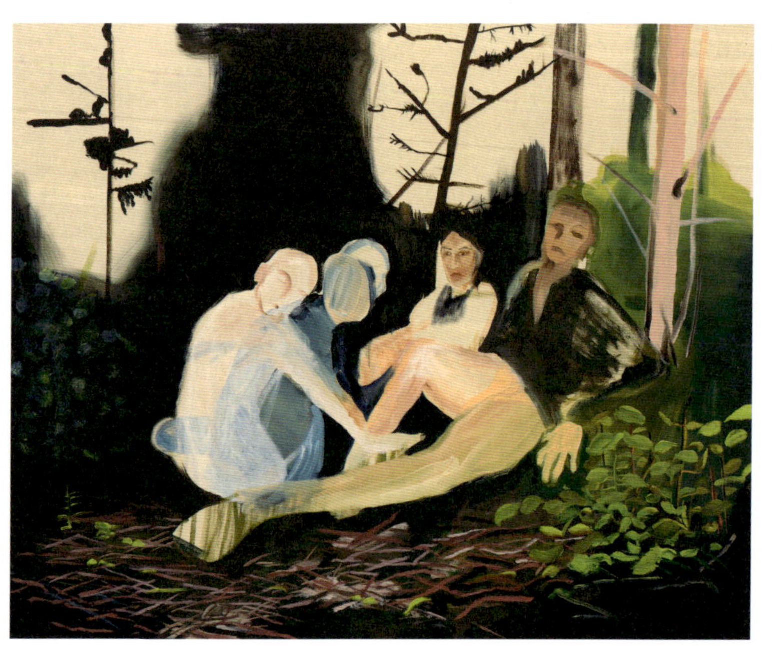

⑥

Bear Trails
2022

BRENDA DRANEY
(b. 1976, member of Sawridge First Nation, Treaty 8; lives/works in Edmonton) proposes painting as a reciprocal relationship between a viewer and artwork. Dream-like, her paintings present a tension between representational specificity and the space of unpainted canvas. Rather than simply represent what has been seen, she renders that which is left unsaid or what is unable to be articulated. Draney's recent notable exhibitions include The Arts Club of Chicago (2023); The Power Plant, Toronto (2023); Catriona Jeffries, Vancouver (2022); McMichael Canadian Art Collection, Vaughan, ON (2020); NS-Dokumentationszentrum, Munich (2019); Walter Phillips Gallery, Banff (2019); Fogo Island Arts, NL (2019); Oakville Galleries, ON (2018); Kitchener-Waterloo Gallery, ON (2017); Audain Gallery, Simon Fraser University, Vancouver (2017); National Gallery of Canada, Ottawa (2016); The Art Gallery of Alberta, Edmonton (2015); and Mendel Art Gallery, Saskatoon (2013). She received her Master's of Applied Arts from Emily Carr University of Art + Design, Vancouver (2010), and her Bachelor's of Fine Arts from the University of Alberta, Edmonton (2006). Draney was the recipient of the Eldon and Anne Foote Visual Arts Prize, Edmonton, in 2014, and she was the winner of the RBC Painting Competition in 2009.

GRAHAM FOY
is a writer and director based in Toronto. His short film *August 22, This Year* (2020) was presented at the Cannes Film Festival's Semaine de la Critique and the New York Film Festival. In 2021, his first feature-film script, "The Maiden," was invited to participate in the Moulin d'Andé residency as part of Cannes's Next Step development program. In 2022, his debut feature *The Maiden* had its world premiere at Giornate degli Autori at the Venice Film Festival, where it received the Cinema of the Future Award. The film continues to tour festivals internationally.

DAVID GARNEAU
(Métis) is Head of Visual Arts at the University of Regina. He is a painter, curator, and critical art writer interested in creative expressions of Indigenous contemporary ways of being. Garneau curated Kahwatsiretátie: The 5th Contemporary Native Art Biennial, Montreal (2020), with assistance from Faye Mullen and rudi aker, and he co-curated, with Kathleen Ash-Milby, *Transformer: Native Art in Light and Sound,* National Museum of the American Indian, New York (2017). Garneau has given keynotes in Australia, New Zealand, the United States, and throughout Canada on issues such as mis/appropriation, re/conciliation, public art, museum displays, and Indigenous contemporary art. His performance, *Dear John,* featuring the spirit of Louis Riel meeting with John A. Macdonald statues, was presented in Regina, Kingston, and Ottawa. In 2021, Garneau installed a large public art work, the *Tawatina Bridge* paintings, in Edmonton. His paintings are in numerous public and private collections.

JACQUELINE KOK
is a curator, a writer, and the Gallery Manager at Empty Gallery,
Hong Kong. From 2021 to 2023, she was the Nancy McCain and Bill
Morneau Curatorial Fellow at The Power Plant, Toronto. During
her term, Kok curated Brenda Draney: *Drink from the river* (2023) and
co-curated the group exhibition *in parallel* (February 3–May 14,
2023). Beyond her current and previous roles, her curatorial projects
span three continents and her writings have appeared in various
publications. Kok's curatorial research pursues the political and social
potentials of space through a deep exploration of the dialectical
relationship among the bodies within it.

KEN LUM
is an artist who has taught at the University of British Columbia,
Vancouver; Bard College, Annandale-on-Hudson, NY; and l'École
nationale supérieure des Beaux-Arts, Paris. He is the co-founder
and founding editor of the *Yishu Journal of Contemporary Chinese
Art*. He delivered keynote addresses at the 2022 International
Association of Empirical Aesthetics Congress, Philadelphia; the
CIMAM 2010 Annual Conference, Shanghai; the 2006 Sydney
Biennale; and the 1997 Universities Art Association of Canada
Conference, Vancouver. His curatorial projects include *Shanghai
Modern: 1919–1945* (2005), the 7th Sharjah Biennial (2005),
and *Monument Lab: Creative Speculations for Philadelphia* (2017).
He was project manager for the exhibition *The Short Century:
Independence and Liberation Movements in Africa, 1945–1994*,
MoMA PS1 (2002). He resides in Philadelphia where he teaches at the
Stuart Weitzman School of Design at the University of Pennsylvania.

JANINE MILEAF
is Executive Director and Chief Curator of The Arts Club of Chicago.
A scholar of the interwar avant-garde, she was formerly Associate
Professor at Swarthmore College, PA. She is the author of *Please
Touch: Dada and Surrealist Objects After the Readymade* (University
Press of New England, 2010) and has co-edited volumes with
Susan Rossen on the history of The Arts Club as well as Chicago
surrealism. At The Arts Club, she has curated exhibitions with such
international artists as Hurvin Anderson, Kerstin Brätsch, Abraham
Cruzvillegas, Suzanne Jackson, Jennie C. Jones, Janice Kerbel,
Hannah Levy, Sharon Lockhart, Josiah McElheny, Jessi Reaves,
Roman Ondak, David Salle, Amy Sillman, and Simon Starling.

SOUVANKHAM THAMMAVONGSA
has had her fiction appear in *The New Yorker, Harper's, Granta,
The Atlantic, The Paris Review, Ploughshares, Best American
Non-Required Reading, The Journey Prize Stories*, and *The O. Henry
Prize Stories*. Her debut book of fiction, *How to Pronounce Knife*,
won the 2020 Scotiabank Giller Prize and was named a finalist for
the National Book Critics Circle Award, the PEN America Open
Book Award, the Danuta Gleed Literary Award, and the Trillium Book
Award, and was one of *Time*'s must-read books of 2020. The title
story was a finalist for the Commonwealth Short Story Prize.

Thammavongsa is also the author of four poetry books: *Light* (2013), winner of the Trillium Book Award for Poetry; *Found* (2007); *Small Arguments* (2003), winner of the ReLit Award; and, most recently, *Cluster* (2019). Born in the Lao refugee camp in Nong Khai, Thailand, she was raised and educated in Toronto, where she is at work on her first novel.

CAROLYN VESELY
is currently the Interim Director of The Power Plant Contemporary Art Gallery, Toronto, and a special arts and culture advisor to the Canadian Urban Institute, Toronto. Prior to joining The Power Plant, Vesely spent more than twenty years at the Ontario Arts Council in roles including CEO, Director of Granting, and Visual and Media Arts Officer, where she was responsible for the funding program that supports Ontario's public art galleries. Vesely has also held several public gallery executive roles, including Director of the Kitchener-Waterloo Art Gallery and Director of the Kelowna Art Gallery.

MARKUS WEISBECK
is a designer and professor of graphic design at the Bauhaus University in Weimar and since 2017 at the Paju Typography Institute in Korea. He has been a member of the Alliance Graphique Internationale since 2011. In 2013, he founded the Space for Visual Research as a workshop and laboratory for experimental research on new graphic and abstract visual worlds, with workshops in China, Taiwan, Korea, Japan, Bolivia, Ecuador, and Iran. Weisbeck's artistic works are represented by Kai Middendorff Gallery, Frankfurt. Studio Markus Weisbeck's projects include work for the Museum für Moderne Kunst, Frankfurt; LUMA Arles; Forsythe Company, Dresden; Zumtobel; Städelschule Architecture Class, Frankfurt; Fogo Island Arts, NL; German Ministry of Finance; Arte, Strasbourg; Deutsche Bank; documenta 12, Kassel; the German Pavilion of the Venice Biennale; Manifesta 7; German Design Council; Sternberg Press; and the German Historical Museum, Berlin.

.30-.30, 2013. Oil on canvas, 121 x 152 cm. Art Gallery of Alberta Collection. Purchased with funds from the John and Maggie Mitchell Endowment Fund and the RCA Trust Grant. Photo: Toni Hafkenscheid.
9 ↗

Evacuation, 2013. Oil on canvas, 91 x 122 cm. Courtesy the artist and Catriona Jeffries, Vancouver. Image courtesy Catriona Jeffries. Photo: Rachel Topham Photography.
10 ↗

Cut, 2022. Oil on canvas, 64 x 51 cm. Commissioned by The Power Plant, 2022. Courtesy the artist and Catriona Jeffries, Vancouver. Image courtesy Catriona Jeffries. Photo: Rachel Topham Photography.
13 ↗

Descendant, 2013. Oil on linen, 122 x 91 cm. Courtesy the artist and Catriona Jeffries, Vancouver. Image courtesy Catriona Jeffries. Photo: Rachel Topham Photography.
14 ↗

Julie, 2010. Oil on linen, 76 x 61 cm. Courtesy the artist and Catriona Jeffries, Vancouver. Image courtesy Catriona Jeffries. Photo: Rachel Topham Photography.
17 ↗

Lawyer, 2022. Oil on canvas, 91 x 122 cm. Commissioned by The Power Plant, 2022. Private collection. Image courtesy Catriona Jeffries, Vancouver. Photo: Rachel Topham Photography.
18 ↗

Legs, 2022. Oil on canvas, 64 x 51 cm. Commissioned by The Power Plant, 2022. Courtesy Joe Friday and Grant Jameson, Ottawa. Image courtesy Catriona Jeffries, Vancouver. Photo: Rachel Topham Photography.
21 ↗

Flood, 2009. Oil on canvas, 122 x 152 cm. Courtesy the artist and Catriona Jeffries, Vancouver. Image courtesy Catriona Jeffries. Photo: Rachel Topham Photography.
22 ↗

Orange Tent, 2020. Oil on canvas, 122 x 152 cm. Collection of John Cook. Image courtesy Catriona Jeffries, Vancouver. Photo: Rachel Topham Photography.
25 ↗

Pray, 2020. Oil on canvas, 64 x 51 cm. Courtesy Michelle Koerner and Kevin Doyle. Image courtesy Catriona Jeffries, Vancouver. Photo: Rachel Topham Photography.
26 ↗

Rest, 2021. Oil on canvas, 196 x 286 cm. Private collection. Image courtesy Catriona Jeffries, Vancouver. Photo: Rachel Topham Photography.
29 ↗

Rose, 2019. Oil on canvas, 91 x 122 cm. Courtesy the artist and Catriona Jeffries, Vancouver. Image courtesy Catriona Jeffries. Photo: Rachel Topham Photography.
30 ↗

Strange Invitation, 2020. Oil on canvas, 122 x 152 cm. Courtesy the artist and Catriona Jeffries, Vancouver. Image courtesy Catriona Jeffries. Photo: Rachel Topham Photography.
33 ↗

Summer Nap, 2017. Oil on linen, 71 x 71 cm. Private collection. Image courtesy Catriona Jeffries, Vancouver. Photo: Toni Hafkenscheid.
34 ↗

Teenager, 2019. Oil on canvas, 51 x 64 cm. Collection of Vicki and Bruce Heyman. Image courtesy Catriona Jeffries, Vancouver. Photo: Rachel Topham Photography.
37 ↗

Toast, 2022. Oil on canvas, 152 x 122 cm. Courtesy the artist and Catriona Jeffries, Vancouver. Image courtesy Catriona Jeffries. Photo: Rachel Topham Photography.
38 ↗

Vanity, 2019. Oil on canvas, 51 x 64 cm. Private collection. Image courtesy Catriona Jeffries, Vancouver. Photo: Rachel Topham Photography.
41 ↗

Visit, 2021. Oil on canvas, 170 x 278 cm. Courtesy Gage and Luke Allard. Image courtesy Catriona Jeffries, Vancouver. Photo: Rachel Topham Photography.
42 ↗

A Basement Party, 2022. Oil on canvas, 170 x 297 cm. Commissioned by The Power Plant, 2022. Courtesy the artist and Catriona Jeffries, Vancouver. Photo: Toni Hafkenscheid.
45 ↗

Dart, 2017. Oil on linen, 71 x 71 cm. Indigenous Art Collection, Crown-Indigenous Relations and Northern Affairs Canada. Photo: Toni Hafkenscheid.
Cover, 46 ↗

Diane, 2022. Oil on canvas, 91 x 91 cm. Commissioned by The Power Plant, 2022. Courtesy the artist and Catriona Jeffries, Vancouver. Photo: Toni Hafkenscheid.
49 ↗

Scroll One, 2010–ongoing. Watercolour and gouache on paper, dimensions variable. Courtesy the artist and Catriona Jeffries, Vancouver. Photo: Toni Hafkenscheid.
50–51 ↗

Self-portrait, 2022. Oil on canvas, 50 x 63 cm. Commissioned by The Power Plant, 2022. Courtesy the artist and Catriona Jeffries, Vancouver. Photo: Toni Hafkenscheid.
52 ↗

Shan, 2013. Oil on canvas, 20 x 25 cm. Payne-Moran Collection. Photo: Toni Hafkenscheid.
55 ↗

Sleep, 2008. Oil on canvas, 40 x 50 cm. Courtesy Alex Hass. Photo: Toni Hafkenscheid.
56 ↗

Tent City, 2010. Oil on canvas, 88 x 106 cm. Private collection. Photo: Toni Hafkenscheid.
59 ↗

The Righteous, 2010. Oil on linen, 50 x 63 cm. Payne-Moran Collection. Photo: Toni Hafkenscheid.
60 ↗

Theatre, 2019. Oil on linen, 157 x 298 cm. Private collection. Photo: Toni Hafkenscheid.
63 ↗

Women, 2017. Oil on canvas, 71 x 71 cm. Courtesy Zita Cobb. Photo: Toni Hafkenscheid.
64 ↗

Accord, 2021. Oil on canvas, 51 x 64 cm. Courtesy the artist and Catriona Jeffries, Vancouver. Image courtesy Catriona Jeffries. Photo: Rachel Topham Photography.
67 ↗

Parish 1–8, 2010. Raku-fired clay, dimensions variable. Courtesy the artist and Catriona Jeffries, Vancouver. Photo: Toni Hafkenscheid.
68 ↗

Tent, 2012. Oil on linen, 91 x 122 cm. Collection of Walter Phillips Gallery, Banff. Image courtesy Catriona Jeffries, Vancouver. Photo: Blaine Campbell.
97 ↗

Vacuum, 2019. Oil on canvas, 91 x 122 cm. Courtesy the artist and Catriona Jeffries, Vancouver. Image courtesy Catriona Jeffries.
97 ↗

Betty, 2012. Oil on canvas, 51 x 64 cm. Courtesy Peggy Garritty. Image courtesy Catriona Jeffries, Vancouver.
98 ↗

Carrie, 2019. Oil on canvas, 221 x 130 cm. Courtesy the artist and Catriona Jeffries, Vancouver. Image courtesy Catriona Jeffries.
99 ↗

Repose, 2013. Oil on canvas, 122 x 91 cm. Collection of Andrew Booth. Image courtesy Catriona Jeffries, Vancouver. Photo: Rachel Topham Photography.
100 ↗

Bear Trails, 2022. Oil on canvas, 122 x 152 cm. Courtesy the artist and Catriona Jeffries, Vancouver. Image courtesy Catriona Jeffries. Photo: Rachel Topham Photography.
100 ↗

This publication was produced in conjunction with Brenda Draney's
exhibition *Drink from the river*, organized and circulated by The
Power Plant Contemporary Art Gallery, Toronto, curated by the
2021–23 Nancy McCain and Bill Morneau Curatorial Fellow
Jacqueline Kok, and presented February 3–May 14, 2023.
The touring venues for *Drink from the river* include The Arts Club
of Chicago, June 14–August 15, 2023, and the Art Gallery of Alberta,
Edmonton, January 22–May 8, 2024.

THE POWER PLANT CONTEMPORARY ART GALLERY

Interim Director: Carolyn Vesely
Head of Curatorial Affairs: Adelina Vlas
Head of Installation and Facilities: Paul Zingrone
Head of Communications and Marketing: Beverly Cheng
Head of Development: William Craddock
Finance Manager: Celia Salas

PUBLICATION

Editors: Adelina Vlas
                                             Jacqueline Kok

Project management: Claudia Tavernese

Texts: Graham Foy
                                             David Garneau
                                             Jacqueline Kok
                                             Ken Lum
                                             Janine Mileaf
                                             Souvankham Thammavongsa
                                             Carolyn Vesely

Copy editing and proofreading: Jack Stanley
                                             Claudia Tavernese

Photography: Blaine Campbell
                                             Toni Hafkenscheid
                                             Rachel Topham

Graphic design: Studio Markus Weisbeck

Printing: Gutenberg Beuys Feindruckerei

Distribution worldwide by Hatje Cantz Verlag GmbH
Mommsenstr. 27
10629 Berlin
Germany
www.hatjecantz.com
A Ganske Publishing Group Company

ISBN 978-3-7757-5593-1

TITLE: Brenda Draney : drink from the river.
OTHER TITLES: Drink from the river
NAMES: Kok, Jacqueline, organizer. | Power Plant (Art gallery), host institution, publisher. |
The Arts Club of Chicago, host institution. | Art Gallery of Alberta, host institution.
DESCRIPTION: This publication was produced in conjunction with Brenda Draney's exhibition
Drink from the river, organized and circulated by The Power Plant Contemporary Art Gallery,
Toronto, curated by Jacqueline Kok, and presented February 3–May 14, 2023. The touring
venues for Drink from the river include The Arts Club of Chicago, June 14–August 15, 2023,
and the Art Gallery of Alberta, Edmonton, January 22–May 8, 2024. | Includes bibliographical
references.
IDENTIFIERS: Canadiana 20230442129 | ISBN 9783775755931 (hardcover)
SUBJECTS: LCSH: Draney, Brenda—Exhibitions. | LCGFT: Exhibition catalogs.
CLASSIFICATION: LCC ND249.D726 A4 2023 | DDC 759.11—dc23

COVER IMAGE: Brenda Draney, *Dart*, 2017. Oil on linen, 71 × 71 cm. Indigenous Art Collection,
Crown-Indigenous Relations and Northern Affairs Canada. Photo: Toni Hafkenscheid.

FRONT AND END PAPERS: Brenda Draney, *Drink from the river*, 2023. Installation views:
The Power Plant Contemporary Art Gallery, Toronto, 2023. Photos: Toni Hafkenscheid.

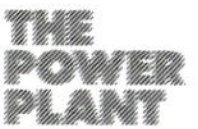 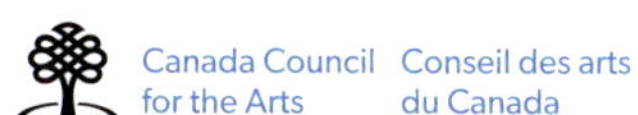 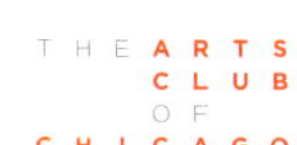 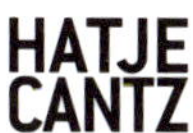 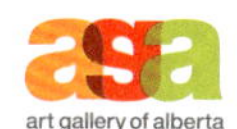

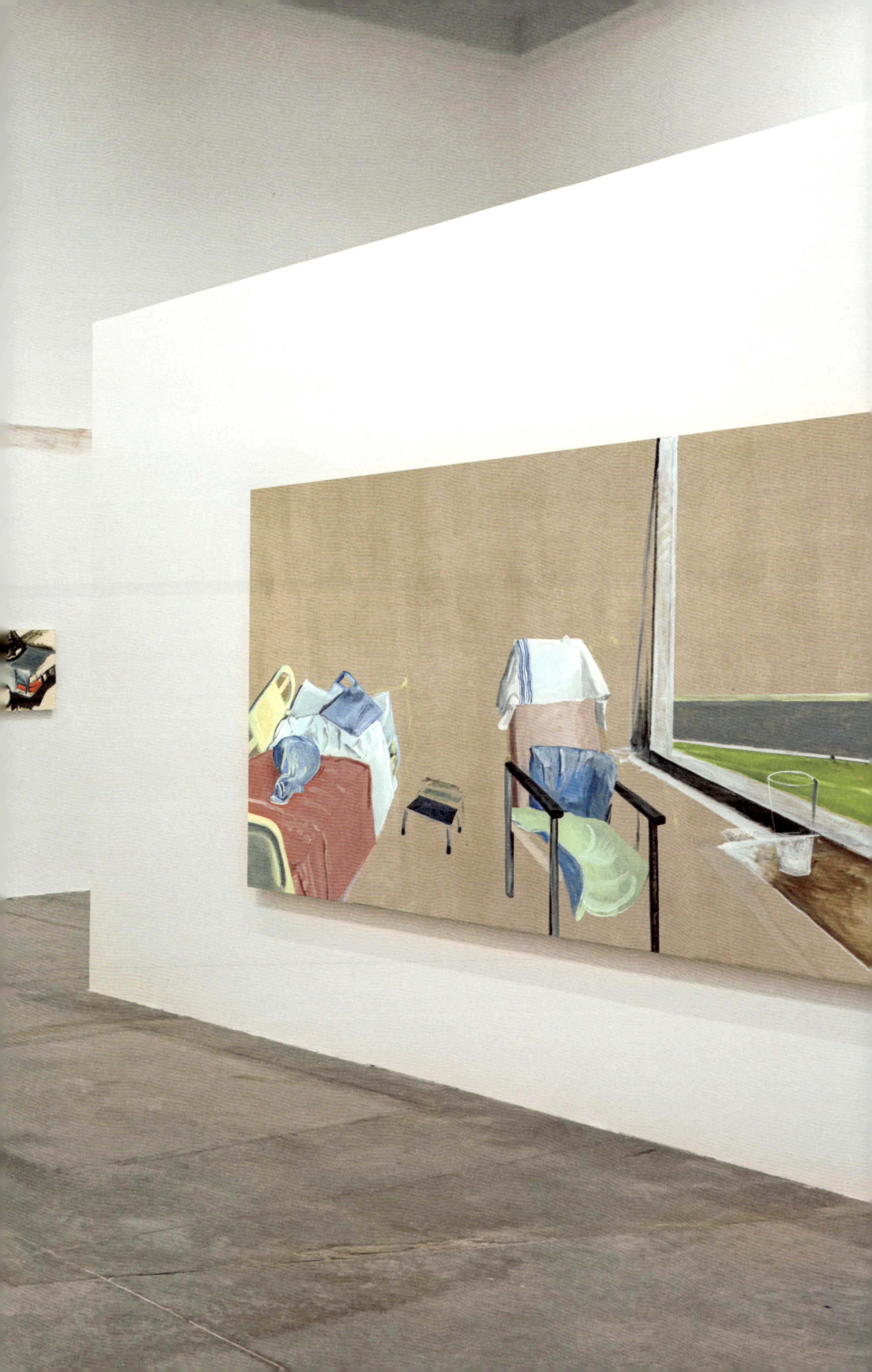

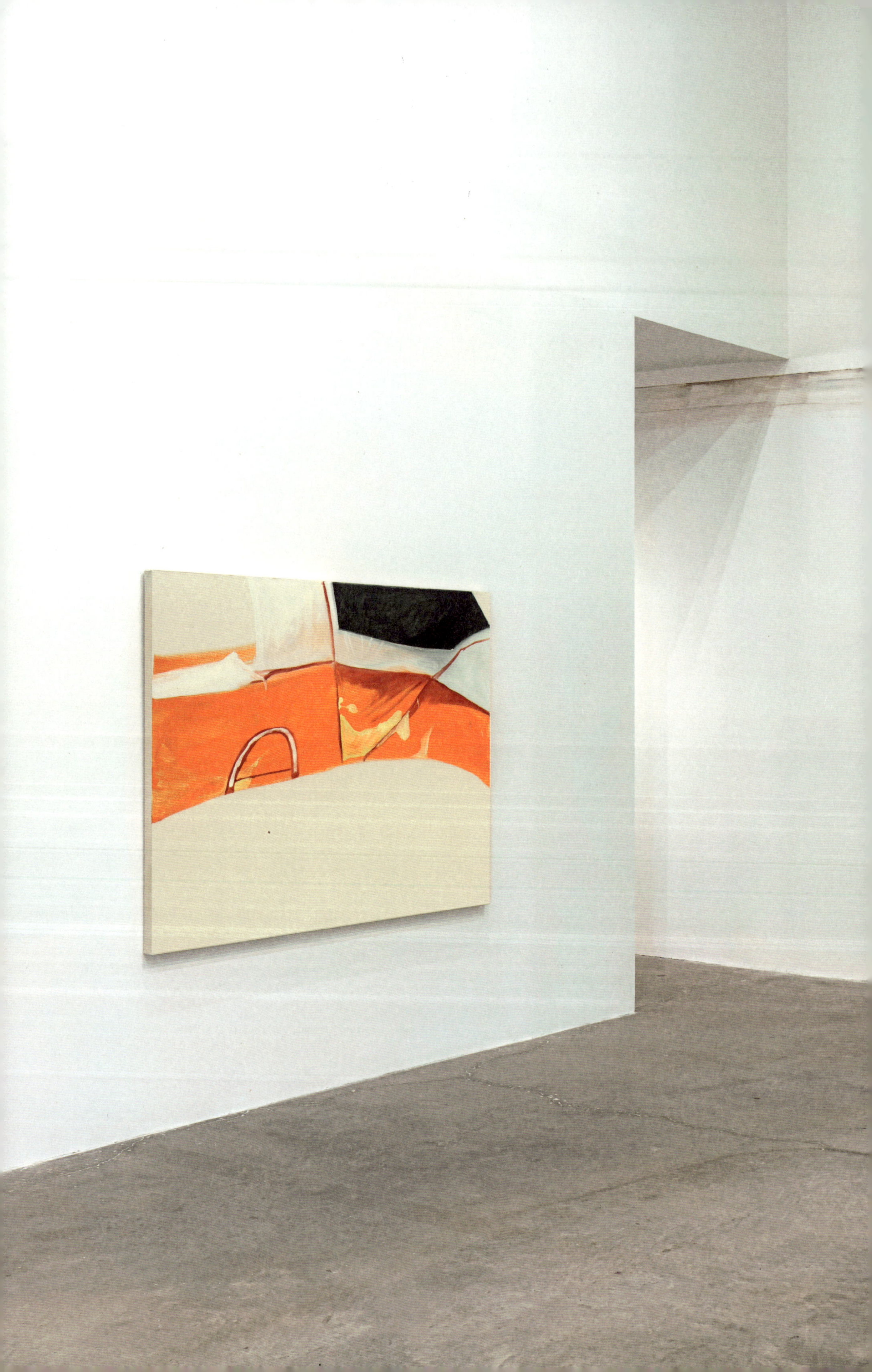

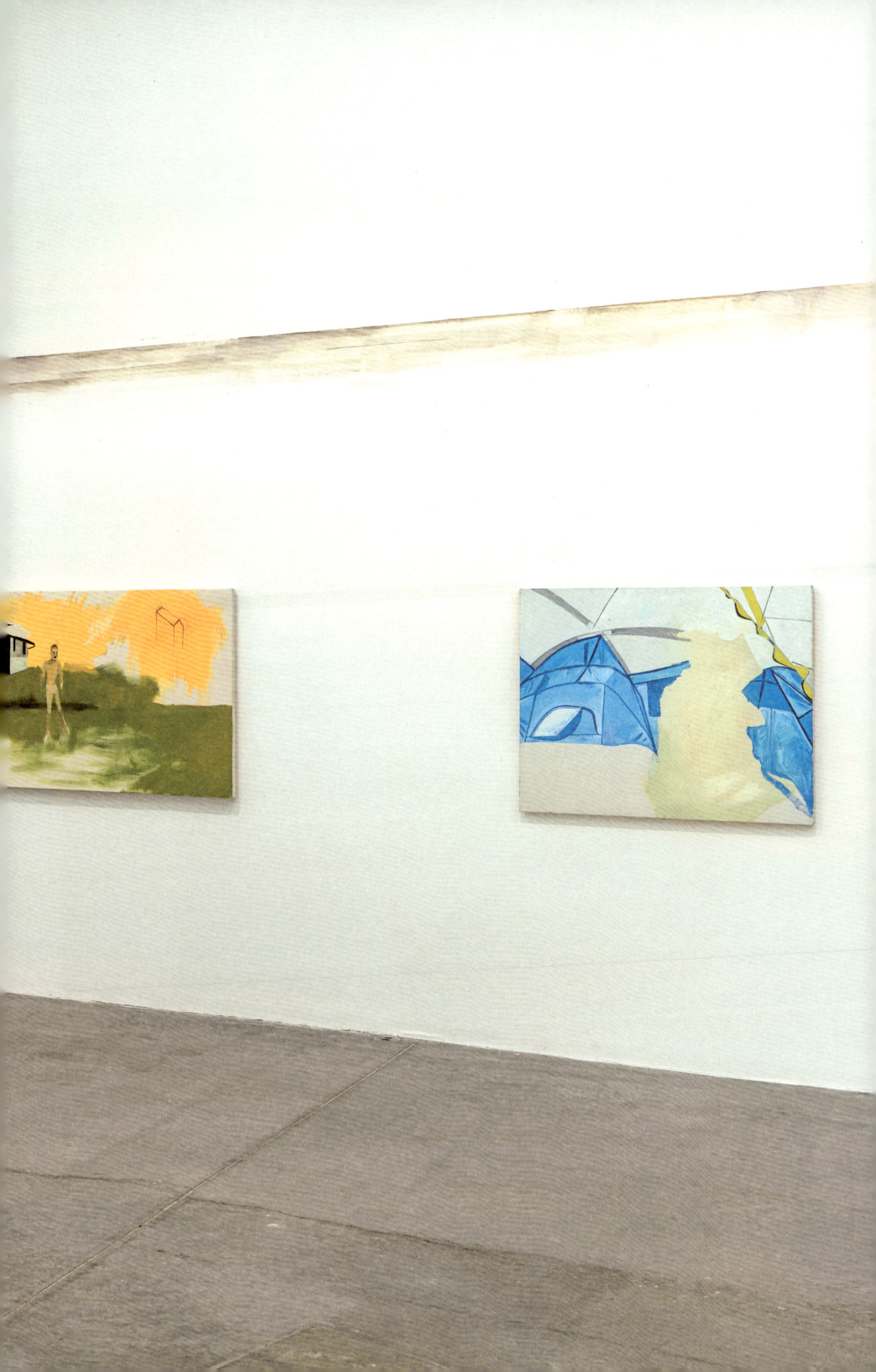

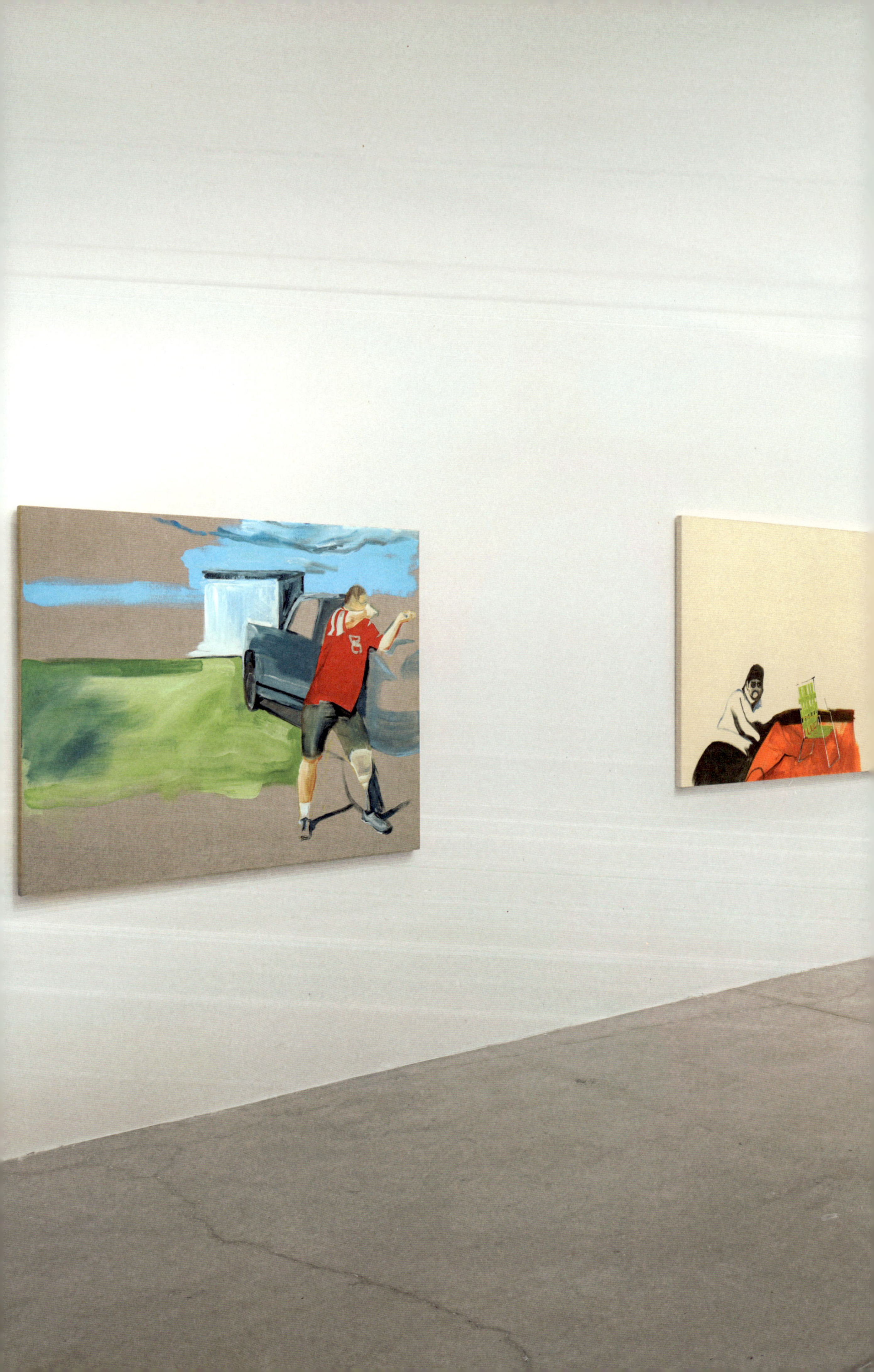

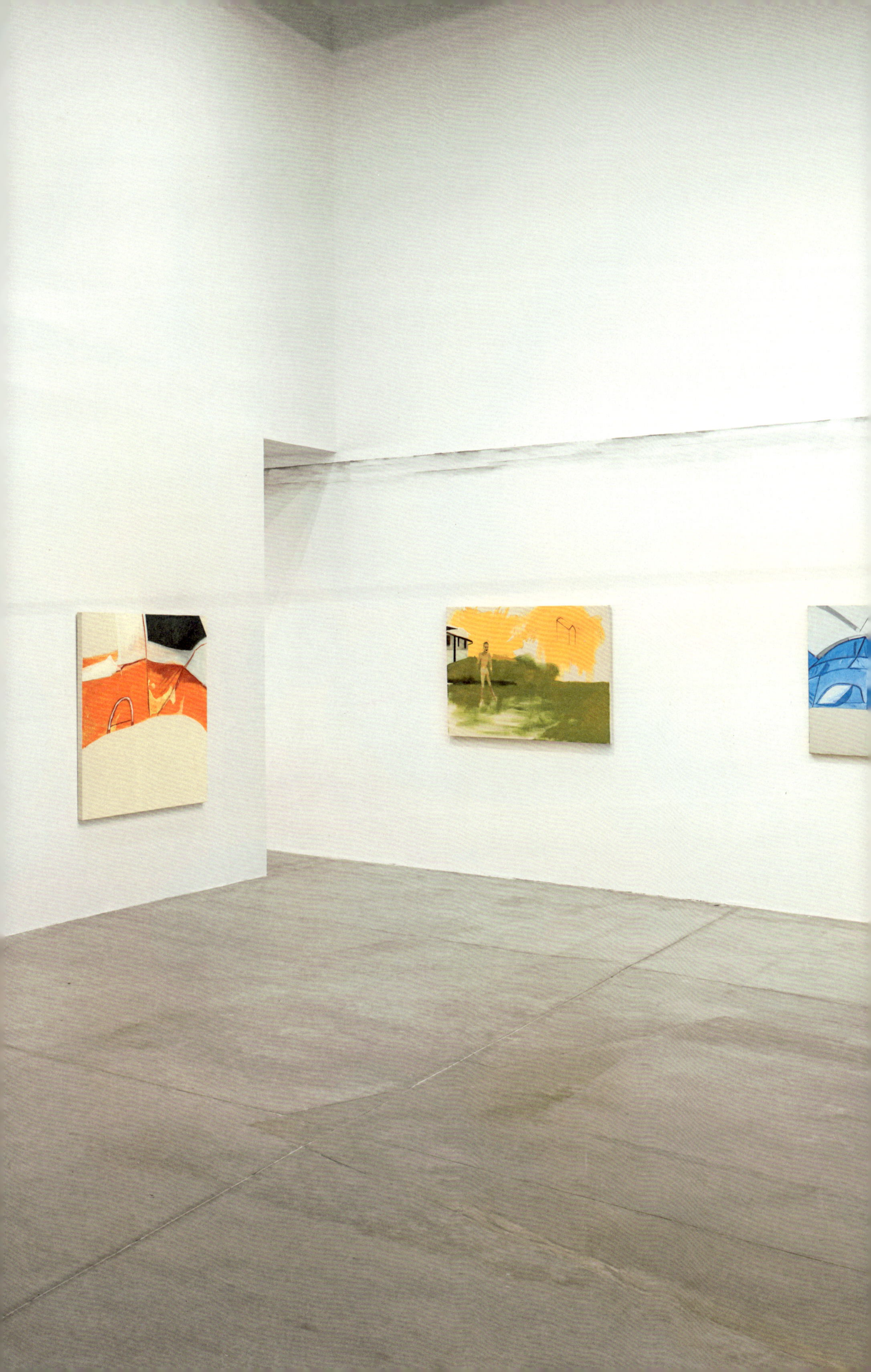

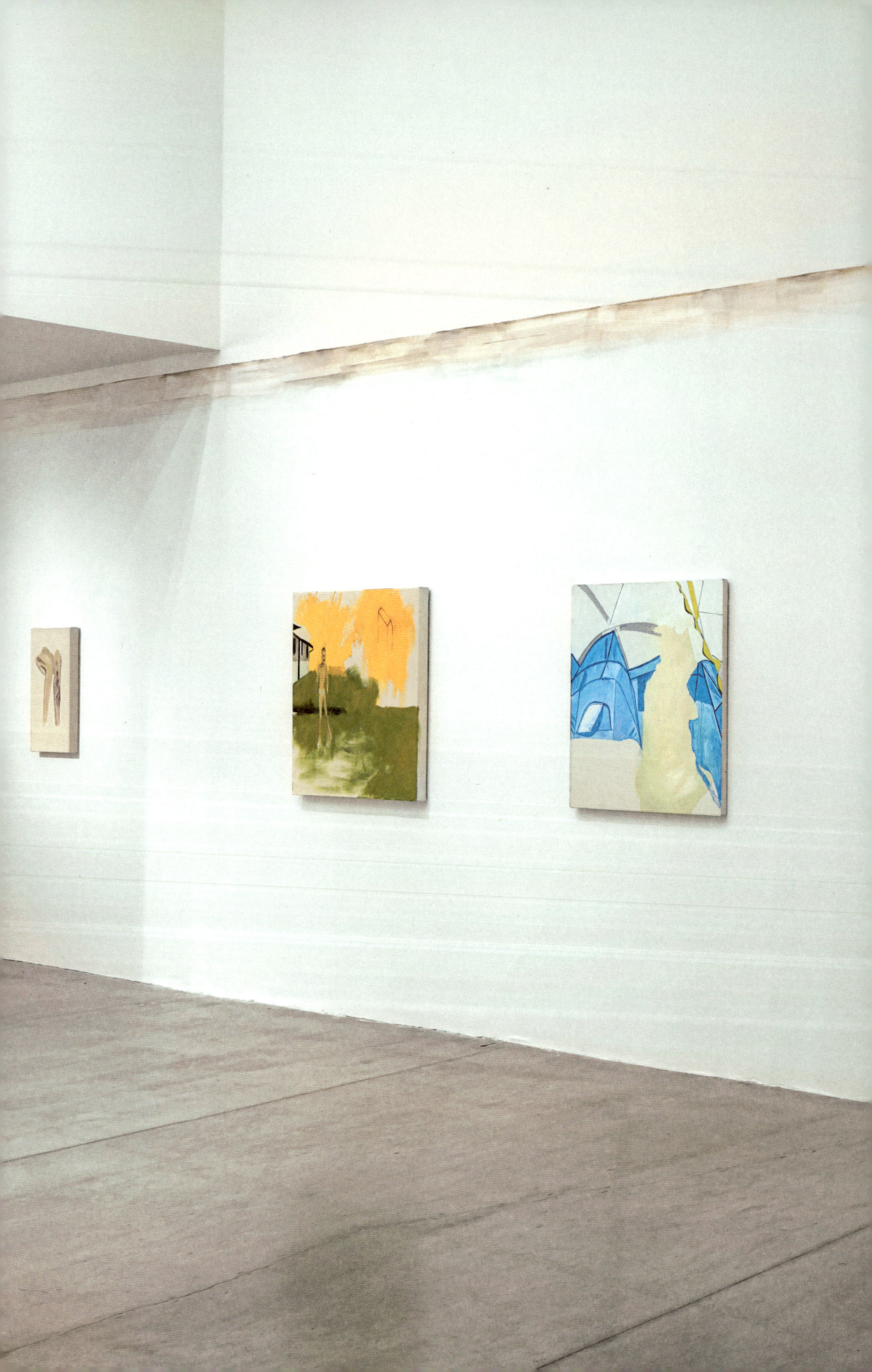

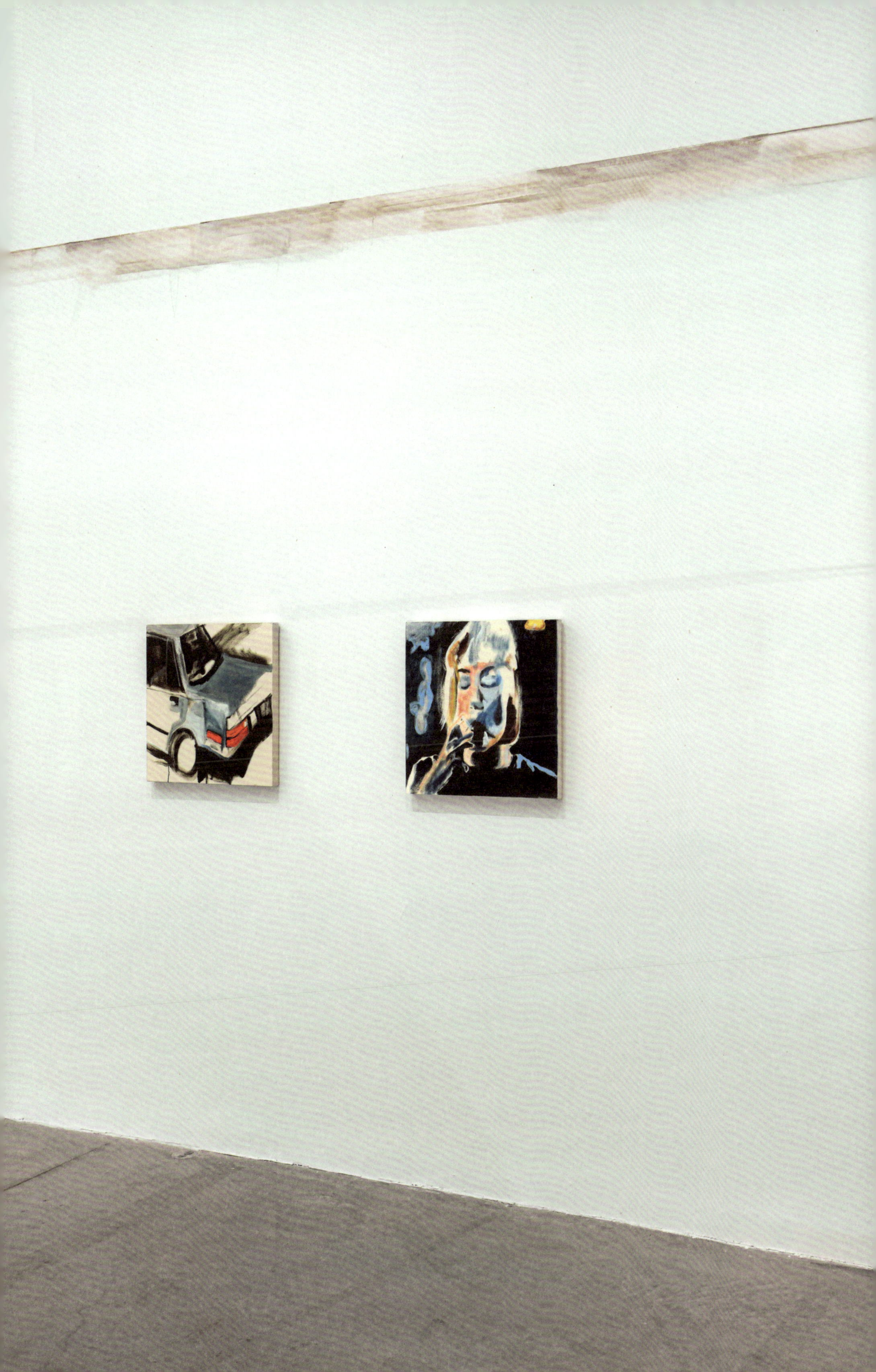

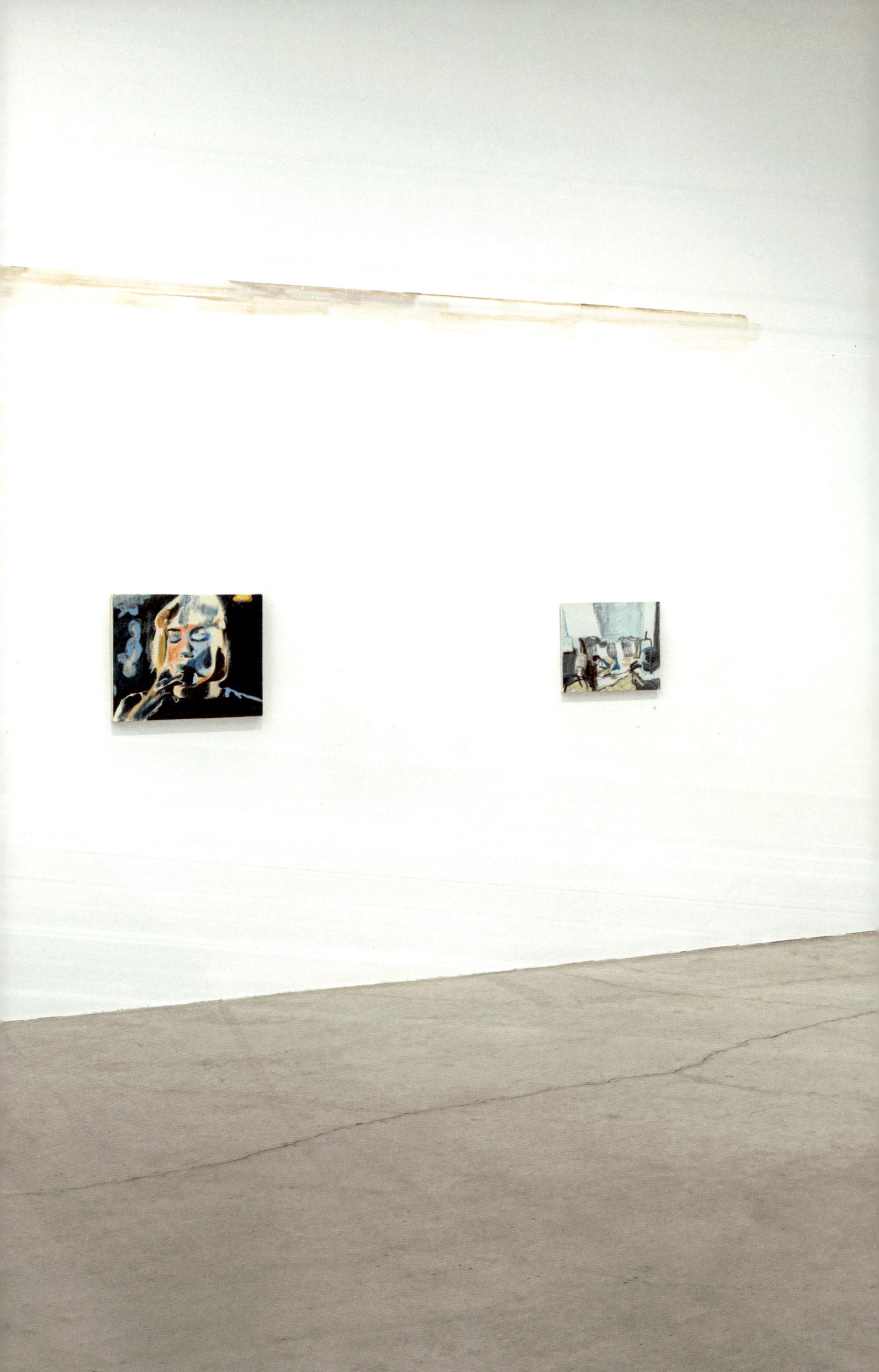

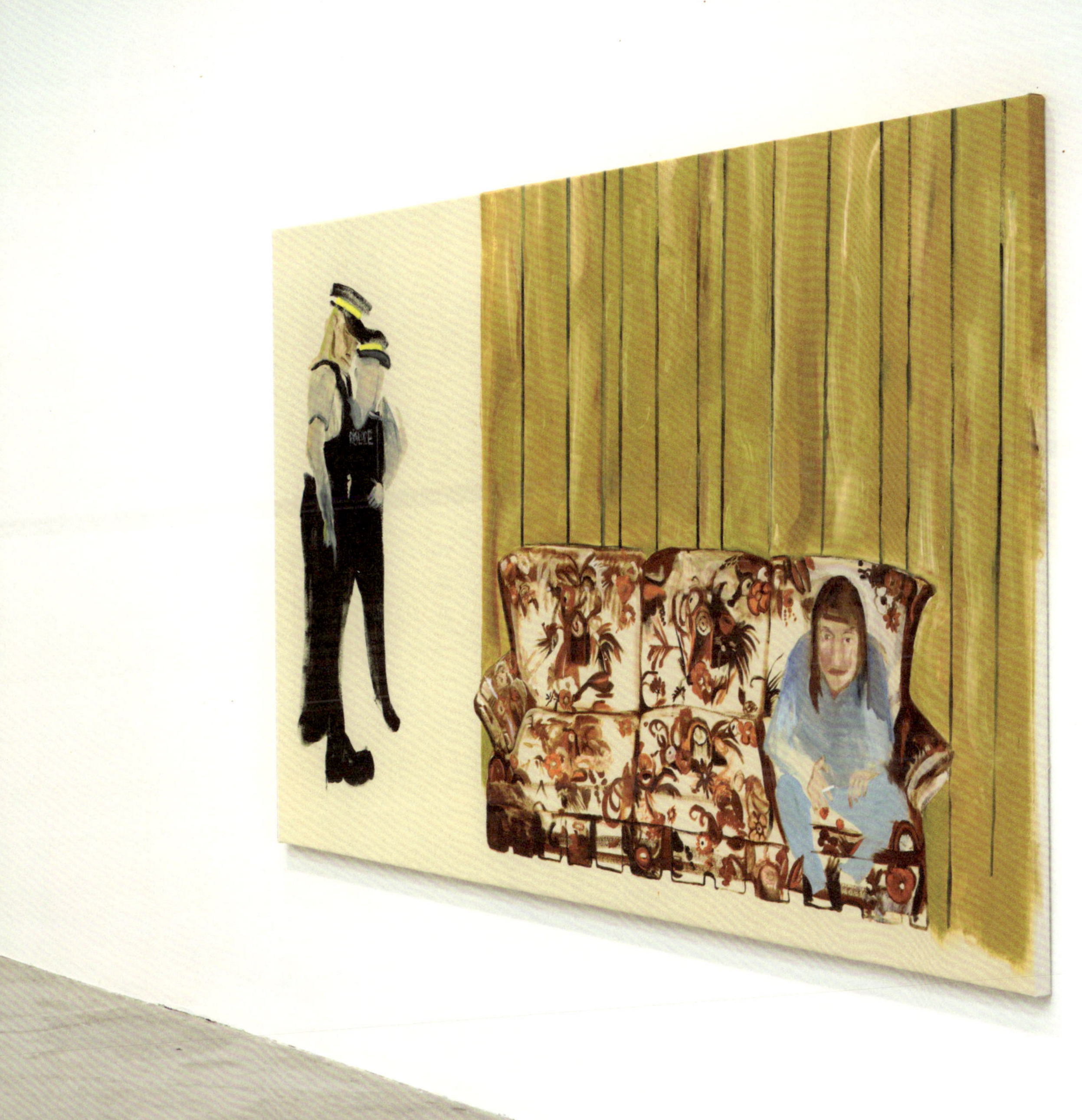

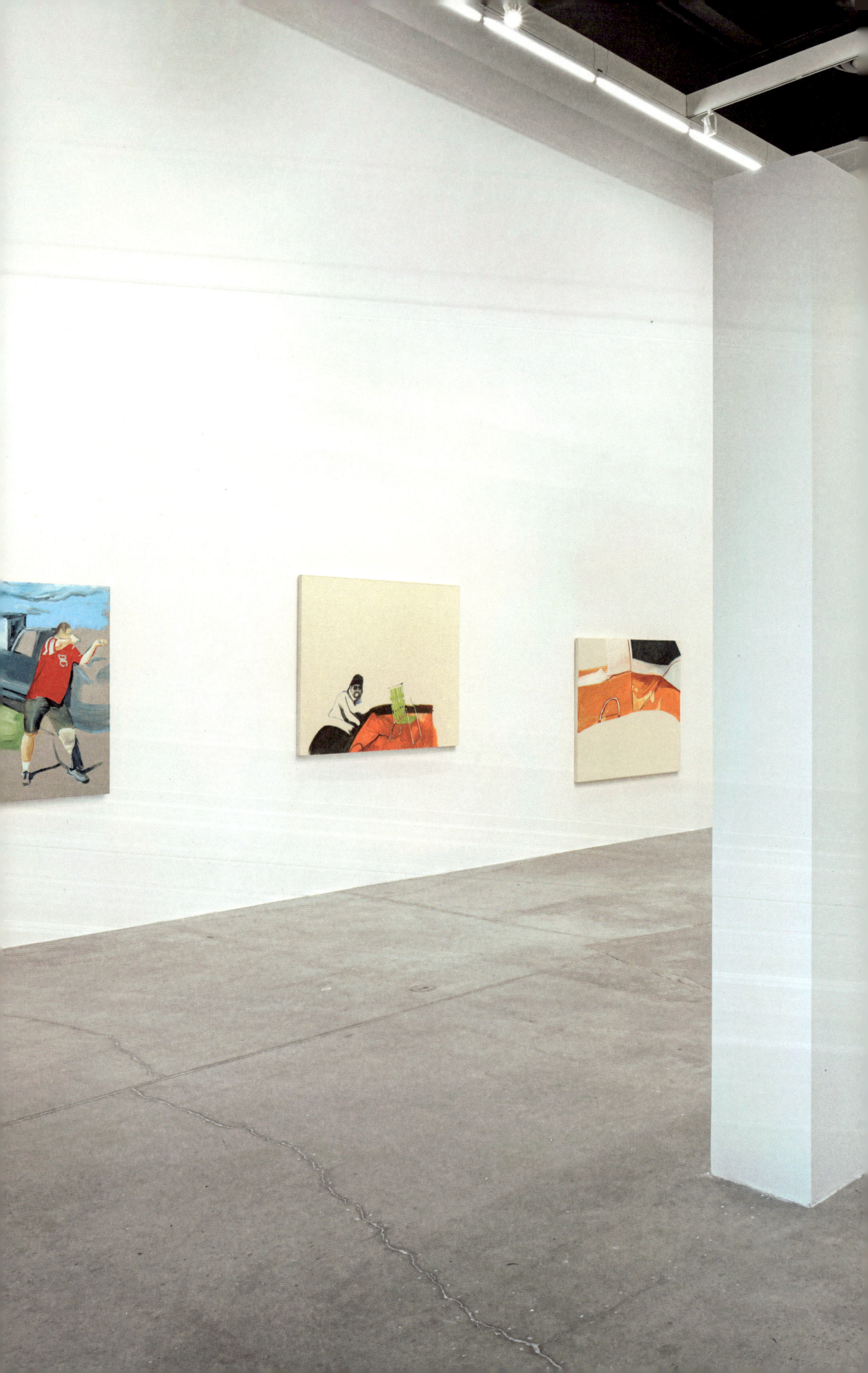

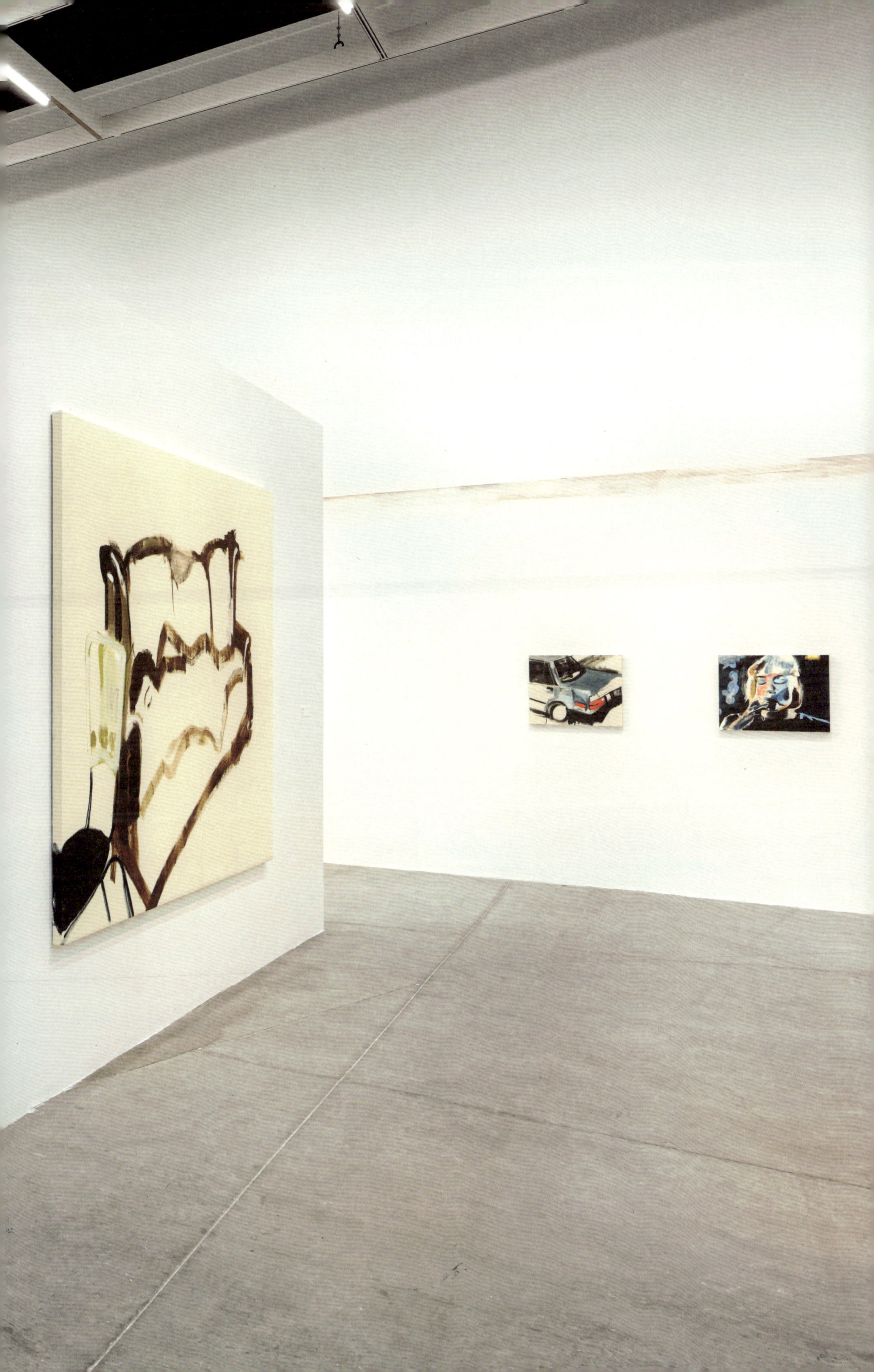

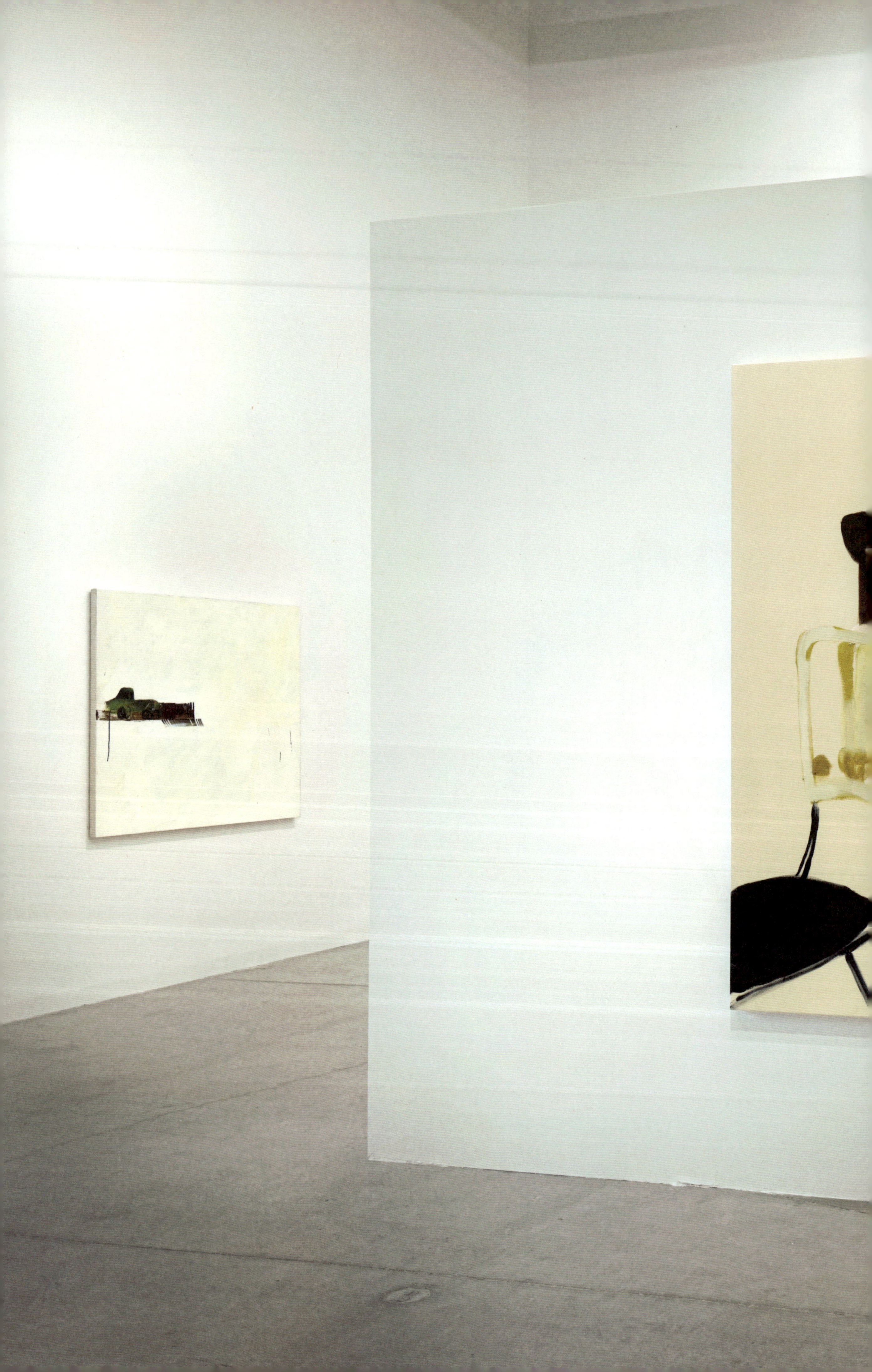

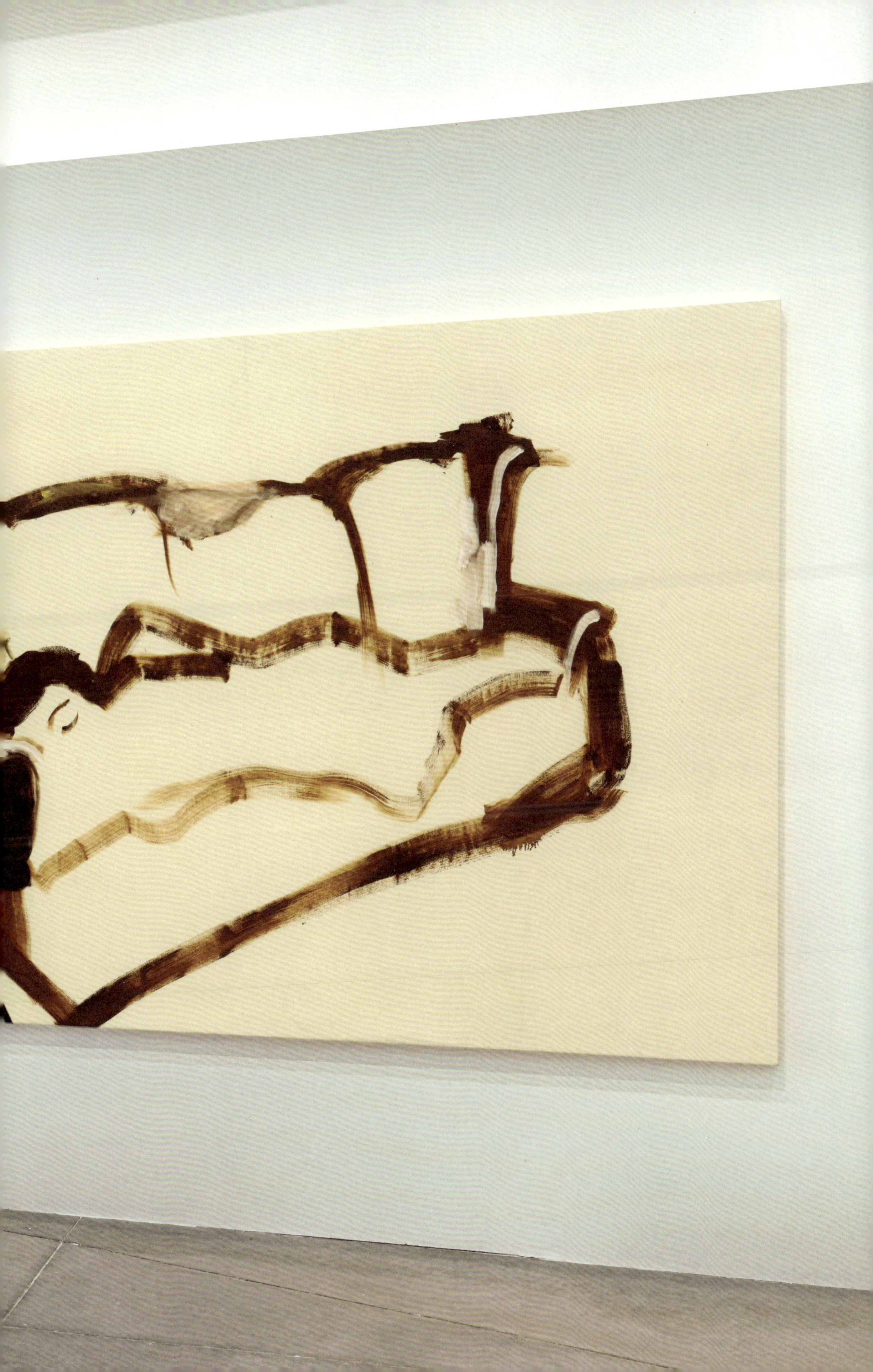

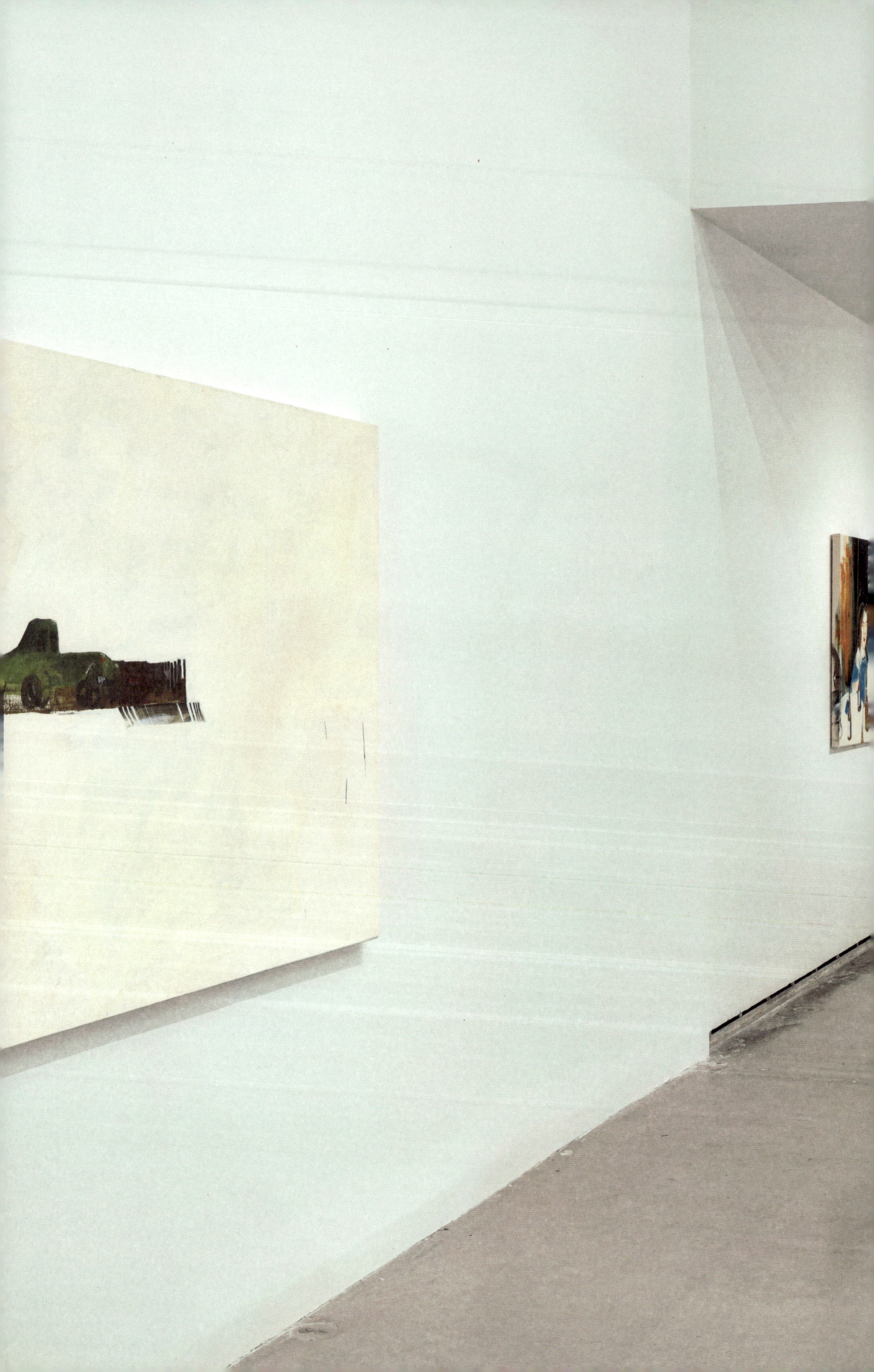